W9-BWI-804

SALTWOOD CASTLE IN WINTER

The castle, with wide views on the north and east to the ridge of the downs, commands the head of a narrow valley down which ran a road to the sea at Hythe. The building here seen did not exist in 1170, but portions of earlier stonework remain. *J. C. Adams, Hythe.*

45707

Thomas Becket

by

DAVID KNOWLES

*Regius Professor Emeritus of Modern History
in the University of Cambridge*

STANFORD UNIVERSITY PRESS
STANFORD, CALIFORNIA
1971

STANFORD UNIVERSITY PRESS
STANFORD, CALIFORNIA

© 1970 BY DAVID KNOWLES

Originating Publisher: A. & C. Black Ltd., London, 1970
First Published in the United States by
Stanford University Press in 1971

Printed in Great Britain

ISBN 0-8047-0766-9

LIBRARY OF CONGRESS CATALOG CARD NO.
771 – 43785

Contents

Illustrations

List of Abbreviations

The following abbreviations of titles of books, etc., are used throughout.

D.N.B.	*Dictionary of National Biography.*
EC.	*The Episcopal Colleagues of Archbishop Thomas Becket*, by David Knowles, Cambridge 1951.
EHD.	*English Historical Documents*, ed. D. C. Douglas, London, 1953–.
EHR.	*English Historical Review.*
GF.	*Gilbert Foliot and his Letters*, by A. Morey and C. N. L. Brooke, Cambridge 1965.
GFL.	*The Letters and Charters of Gilbert Foliot*, edd. A. Morey and C. N. L. Brooke, Cambridge 1967.
GW.	*Guernes de Pont-Sainte-Maxence*, ed. E. Walberg, Lund 1922.
JS.	*The Letters of John of Salisbury*, i (1153–61), edd. W. J. Millor, H. E. Butler and C. N. L. Brooke, London 1955.
MB.	*Materials for the History of Thomas Becket, Archbishop of Canterbury*, edd. J. C. Robertson (i–vi) and J. B. Sheppard (vii), Rolls Series 67, London 1875–85.
	Throughout the book these vols. have been cited by number of volume, number of item (in brackets) for the letters in v–vii, and page in the RS., e.g. *MB.*, vii. (746), 451.
RS.	Rolls Series. 'Chronicles and Memorials of Great Britain and Ireland during the Middle Ages'. H.M. Stationery Office, London.
Thómas Saga.	*Thómas saga erkibyskups*, ed. E. Magnússon, 2 vols. (RS. 65), London 1875–83.
TL.	*Thomas of London before his Consecration*, by L. B. Radford, Cambridge 1894.

Foreword

ANYONE who undertakes to write a short life of St Thomas of Canterbury has to face a number of difficulties. One is provided by the mass of biographical and other material that must be examined, another by the number of topics that demand for their understanding a familiarity with distant origins as well as with recent precedents, and with the slow movements of law and custom; and a third by the difficulties of interpretation that surround the actions of the archbishop and his opponents. No saint has made a greater impact upon the public life of the England of his day, but this impact was on the external, secular level, whereas his private and spiritual life is more dimly seen. Indeed, his canonization and his posthumous fame were directly and solely due to his martyrdom.

I have endeavoured to meet these difficulties by a close adherence to the sources, by a relatively lengthy examination of the pre-history of the controversies in which Thomas was involved, and by an endeavour to see the archbishop in the context of his age. From the day of his death to the sixteenth century he was a figure of majesty, abiding no question. In the latter part of the reign of Henry VIII he became and remained a highly controversial figure, a turbulent and fanatical priest to some, an admirable confessor and martyr to others. The division, originally between Catholics and Protestants, became later one between historians who admired Henry II, and admirers of Thomas of all creeds, who saw in him a defender of spiritual principle against secular tyranny. On the whole, popular favour has abandoned the archbishop, and many in print, and more in conversational judgment, have expressed a distaste for what they regard as his violent and ambitious character. Nevertheless, his story continues to occupy a place among the most familiar episodes of English history. No other has been more frequently celebrated in art of every kind and in every kind of drama, and it is safe to say that no other English saint, whether in the thirteenth century or in 1970, could attract to his shrine, whether still adorned with gold and precious stones or eloquent by its empty site, the multitudes 'from every shire's end' who have visited Canterbury.

The twelfth century was an age of great men in every sphere of activity: kings, bishops, abbots, thinkers, administrators, architects, illuminators, sculptors, biographers and historians. England alone gave birth in that age to more saints than in any other century, and created monuments in stone that still draw visitors by the thousand, and institutions that survive to our own day. So rich is the variety of interest that many who write of St Thomas in exile in France can be oblivious of the seething currents of thought and religious fervour—the recovery of Aristotle, the *Concordia* of Gratian, the *Sentences* of the Lombard, the building of Sens and Chartres and Laon—that were eddying round him. Historians, architects and antiquaries have restored to us his Canterbury, so that we can see each narrow street with its houses and their tenants—Canterbury, laced by the elusive waters of the Stour, grouped about the walled precincts of its two great ministers, its cathedral far-seen by pilgrims and travellers from or to the Continent as they first caught sight of the city in its wide valley. Pontigny, his first refuge, stands still in much of its original purity of design, the church and cloister where the archbishop and his clerks spent their most bitter months, now lonely amid the fields and their background of trees. Sens, the third church associated with his story, may well have seen him assisting at the consecration of its high altar by Alexander III, while the architect of its nave, William of Sens, was to repeat his achievement more than a decade later at Canterbury. We think, rightly, of the hardships of the archbishop's exile, but they were years spent in what was to many Englishmen the most delightful region of the world, the heartland of France, the 'sweet France' of Herbert of Bosham and John of Salisbury.

Twenty years ago I spent many months with Thomas, his colleagues, his correspondents and his biographers. Returning to the same sources for another year, I tried to avoid reading either my own or other recent accounts of the events and problems of that time. If despite this the judgments and even the language of this book sometimes resemble those of earlier years the reader must believe me that this is because the same documents have still made the same impression on my mind.

My thanks are due to the General Editor, Professor C. W. Dugmore, both for his original invitation and for his indulgence in awaiting a tangible result. They are also eminently due to

Professor C. N. L. Brooke, for his criticisms and help throughout
the making of this book. It is now twenty-five years since he
first gave generously of his time to removing errors from my
typescripts and proofs. He was then an undergraduate; he is
now a Fellow of the British Academy. But he must not be held
responsible for errors and questionable judgments that remain.
I am grateful to Lord Clark of Saltwood and to Dr J. K. St Joseph
for providing photographs of Saltwood Castle and Clarendon, to
Dr William Urry for permission to use his plan of the precinct
of Canterbury on 29 December, 1170, and to the publishers for
allowing the illustrations, and for many other courtesies.

13 *July*, 1970   DAVID KNOWLES

CHAPTER I

Thomas of London

THE long quarrel between King Henry II and Archbishop Thomas Becket, culminating in the murder of the archbishop in Canterbury cathedral, is one of the most familiar episodes in English history. The immediate and lasting consequence, the creation of a cult that made of Canterbury one of the three most celebrated goals of European pilgrimage in the later middle ages, and the wealth of detail concerning the last days and minutes of the archbishop's life contributed by a galaxy of contemporary biographers, combined to engrave what may be called the saga of Thomas Becket deeply upon the imagination of Europe. Countless representations of the murder in manuscripts, on panels and in stone, carried the story from churches and monasteries into the homes and folk-lore of the people. In the modern world the tale has been taken up by poets and dramatists, to say nothing of writers of popular history and religious controversy. It has been filmed and televised, and without a doubt it will continue to inspire a regular succession of works of art and imagination in the future.

The story of Thomas Becket has this fascination by reason of its clear-cut theme of a firm friendship turning to bitter enmity and crowned by a heroic death. On a deeper level, also, it has a powerful appeal, when it is conceived as the resistance of spiritual leadership to secular domination or, reversing the picture, as the endeavour of a reforming monarch to overcome obscurantist and fanatical opposition. While the former presentation was given spectacular encouragement by the public penance of the king, by the wonders worked at the martyr's tomb and by the immediate canonization of the victim, with a feast-day within the octave of Christmas, the latter outlook came into prominence when another King Henry disembarrassed himself of another

Thomas, his sometime chancellor and friend, and razed every visible monument of Becket from the churches and books of his subjects; and this attitude has been prolonged not only by the fires of religious controversy, but also by the searchlights of critical historians. Finally, the episode has been raised above the dust of controversy by recent work on the whole body politic of England in the twelfth century and on the relation of the quarrel to the deeper issues of spiritual dominion and secular government in the Europe of Becket's day.

Yet, despite all that has been written, a diversity of opinion remains as to the character of Thomas, the nature of the quarrel and the legal and spiritual issues at stake. As to the character of the archbishop, all criticism was barred for almost four centuries. The martyrdom, the miracles and the canonization, backed by the united testimony of all the biographers, gave the saint an intangible position until the reign of Henry VIII. Then, without any new evidence coming to light, opinion divided sharply along confessional lines which, though becoming slightly blurred, remained visible even in our own time. Similarly, the nature of the quarrel was interpreted differently before and after the sixteenth century. Before that, it was understood as the saint's biographers saw it: that is, as an attack by the royal government upon the rights of the Church. The fact that the secular power had never fully accepted this view and, indeed, had again and again taken up in practice an entirely contrary attitude had no influence on the literary tradition, which was a monopoly of monks and clerics during the middle ages. The Reformation had the effect of ending for long all serious study of medieval English saints, and the Bollandists, after more than three hundred years of labour on the lives of the saints, day by day throughout the year, are still some seven weeks away from 29 December, and there is little hope that they will reach that date in the present century. When a new critical approach to history began in the nineteenth century Becket was once more a figure of religious controversy, but when Maitland had made clear the great achievement of Henry II and his servants in centralising and clarifying English civil and criminal legal procedure, the sympathies of historians turned to the king. Canonical and spiritual issues were only touched lightly, and along conventional lines, till very recently, and no attempt was made to set the technical issues of the quarrel in their place as elements in the long evolution of Christian thought and law affecting the claims of the Church to be regarded as an autonomous society on the one hand, and the natural and, indeed, indefeasible claims of the civil government to judge and control its subjects in matters of social and material activity.

Thomas was born on the feast-day of the apostle of that name, 21 December, probably in 1118. He was born at a house in Cheapside in the city of London, perhaps the first of England's great men to be essentially and professedly a Londoner. His father was a London merchant and for a time sheriff of the city, but Gilbert Becket, whose name is found in one of the few documents of the age connected with London,[1] was by birth a Norman from Rouen. His mother, Roesa or Matilda, was a native of Caen. Gilbert, or possibly his father, was one of the numerous Norman adventurers who came to England after the Conquest, and as Rouen was to Normandy what London was to south-east England, the chief port of entry and commercial capital, migration from one to the other was natural. Thomas was, thus, of pure Norman blood. The myth of Anglo-Saxon parentage, which has bedevilled both history and drama, has no vestige of support in the historical evidence. His father, according to one of Thomas's biographers, was of knightly family, a distinction which both in classical Latin and modern English gives the reader a misleading class-mark. The knight (Anglo-Saxon *cniht*, a servant) was a military follower of a feudal tenant, and one substantial enough to possess a horse and chain mail, but not till shortly before 1100 did such knights begin to disperse from their lords' households to rural smallholdings. The son of such a father would not in the early twelfth century degrade himself by entering into trade. Gilbert Becket, as the sources tell us, entertained at his house friends of knightly and higher social groups. At the time of Thomas's birth, indeed, the distinction was not between landed knight and city burgess, but between Norman and English, and here the young Thomas could and did feel a solidarity with the Norman conquerors who throughout his life, though in ever-decreasing measure, were the dominant stratum of society in the king's court, and in the

1. English translation in *EHD.*, ii. 953 (277). For the early life of Thomas (1118–54), with copious references, see *TL.*

castles, cathedrals and abbeys of the land. He could, in later life, feel completely at ease with the outlook and loyalties of the feudal barons.

As regards his name, the family surname was in general restricted to the Norman feudatories who carried their territorial distinctions across the Channel and imposed them far and wide upon the English countryside from Thorpe Mandeville to Norton Fitzwarren. At the lower end of the social scale, which was also below the level of literacy, the Christian name alone reached the records, though in the relationships of daily life an employment such as a smith's probably added a distinguishing mark. Between the highest and the lowest, the place of origin was used for identification when individuals left home, an identification which was all the more needed on account of the paucity of Christian names in common use. 'Becket' was probably a nickname of Gilbert which would have stuck to his son as a town-dweller. As soon as he left his parents' home the name of Thomas of London was used; it would have been of little significance on Cheapside. Certainly it was his usual appellation until he held high office when he became Thomas of Canterbury, though Becket was still very occasionally used by contemporaries, perhaps with a slightly derogatory implication.[1]

The London in which Thomas Becket was born and bred was already an important place. Cities are great not merely by reason of population. Many of the cities of to-day touching or passing the million mark are little more than a vast congeries of houses, flats, offices, shops, factories and warehouses. Neither now nor in the past have they harboured citizens of genius; they have themselves no *genius loci*. Others, with far smaller population, have had many eminent citizens whom they have stamped with their own characteristics. London, from Roman times to the present, has always been the metropolis of England, though of the various elements that combine to make a city great—a royal court, the seat of government, a cathedral with its entourage, a home of academic life, the national courts of law, a national port and mart—only the last has been a part of London's greatness

---

1. In the voluminous correspondence and biographies of *MB.*, it is used only twice, viz., ii. 435, by the knights calling angrily in the cathedral, and by the Grandimontine Peter Bernard, using the unfamiliar phrase 'reverendus ille pater Becket', *MB.*, vii. (746), 451. 'Becket' = little beak.

from the beginning to the present day. London made and retained its celebrity as the centre of national merchantry and finance. Since the eleventh century it has been powerfully assisted by the presence of the court and some of the organs of government in the neighbouring Westminster, but in the twelfth century, as indeed at the present time also, what is technically the city of London had its chief interest and skill in finance and commerce.

The prosperity of London received a great impetus from the Norman Conquest. By its immediate surrender it escaped any kind of destruction or penalization, and was very soon enriched by the influx of merchants and men of substance from Normandy. In the eleventh and early twelfth centuries an exclusive class distinction did not yet exist to draw a line, not only between the aristocracy and the commoner, but also between the higher churchmen and lawyers, and the merchant or wealthy wholesaler or tradesmen of the city. The latter, indeed, in London at least had a higher literacy and competence in finance and the skills of municipal government than many of the higher orders. The leading citizens of London ranked as barons, a term which has no modern equivalent, but which, with all necessary adjustments to different circumstances, had something of the significance of patrician rank in ancient Rome or medieval Venice.

The celebrated description of London by William FitzStephen,[1] one of Archbishop Thomas's clerks, was written *circa* 1173, but probably represents the picture in the writer's memory of the city as it was twenty or thirty years earlier. It is the first clear glimpse of England's capital, and it was long before another equally vivid picture was drawn. Our imagination lingers over his description of the public restaurant near the river which included in its scope expensive dishes of a Lucullan luxury and hot packed meals to take away for the benefit of citizens on whom an unexpected guest had called. FitzStephen dilates upon the thirteen major churches and the 126 smaller ones. Some of these would have been proprietary churches, constructed by one or more citizens of consequence for their private devotional use. During Thomas's boyhood London, first among the towns of England, enjoyed a measure of self-government, with a sheriff and a justiciar, and the right to render the farm of London and Middlesex, though its privileges were reduced under Stephen

1. *MB.*, iii. 2–13. English translation in *EHD.*, ii. 956–62 (281).

and Henry II.[1] Already in Thomas's time, prelates and magnates had town houses in London; it was these that helped to provide the link-up of building along a line from Ludgate to Westminster Abbey.

The mother of a saint usually receives an exaggerated meed of praise from hagiographers, but we can accept the testimony of those who knew Thomas well that his mother was devout, and that he owed to her a grounding in the Christian faith and devotion to the Mother of God,[2] even if we prune away the signs and wonders that presaged his sanctity. He had at least three sisters: Mary, a nun of Barking who ultimately became abbess; Agnes, the foundress of St Thomas's Hospital; and Roesia; and at least four nephews: Ralph and John, sons of Roesia, Gilbert and Geoffrey.[3] The two last-named were cousins, but we have no indication of their relationship to Ralph, so it is possible that Gilbert was a son of Roesia and Geoffrey of Agnes. There is no suggestion in any of the biographies that any of his sisters had a significant place in his early life or later, though they were to suffer on account of their relationship.

At the age of ten Thomas was given by his father into the care of Robert, prior of the Augustinian canons of Merton, a recent (1117) foundation of Henry I. Another Robert, a canon of the house, was his confessor and confidant in after life.[4] Merton has suffered more than most monastic sites from urban and industrial invasion, but it was a house of great influence, the founding mother of at least seven others. A small grass enclosure, indicated

1. *EHD.*, ii. 946–7 (271).
2. John of Salisbury vouches for this, *MB.*, ii. 302–3: 'sicut referre solitus est [Thomas]'.
3. Mary was appointed by the king 'on account of her brother' in 1173 (R. Diceto, RS., i. 371), at the suggestion of Prior Odo of Canterbury (Gervase of Canterbury, *Chronicle*, RS., i. 242). Guernes knew her well (*GW.*, pp. 210–11). For Agnes, see Sir William Dugdale, *Monasticon Anglicanum*, vi. 646–7. Roesia, whose pardon was begged by King Henry in July 1174, was given the profits of the King's Mill at Canterbury as recompense for her sufferings in exile (W. Urry, *Canterbury under the Angevin Kings*, London, 1967, 182). For her sons John and Ralph, see *ibid.*, index *s. vv.* For Geoffrey and Gilbert, who were cousins, see *MB.*, v. (138), 248; vi. (449), 485–6 (Gilbert); and v. (55), 102; vi. (405, 449), 397, 485 (Geoffrey, then a poor scholar).
4. Many writers, including J. C. Robertson (*MB.*, index vi. 675) have confused Prior Robert I of Merton (d. 1150), or Prior Robert II, with the canon, Robert, who survived the archbishop.

by excavations forty years ago as marking the site of the high altar, lies between the steel and glass constructions of a modern factory, with tall chimneys, and the track of a suburban railway, but the station which once lay at the east end of the church is now derelict, after a life even shorter than the monastic buildings it replaced. The Wandle brook, which once served to cleanse the offices of the priory, now flows in undignified confinement, its waters soiled by industrial effluvia and the foam of detergents. Nothing whatever is left of the house and church that Thomas knew, but it undoubtedly had a formative influence upon him, and when he became archbishop he returned thither to take the habit of a canon.

Merton served only as a preparatory school, and after a few years Thomas entered one of the three principal schools of London, possibly that of St Paul's. His biographer notes that inter-school competitions in dispute and declamation existed already, as also the sports of cock-fighting and football, which even then attracted crowds from the city to the fields outside the northern wall. From the London grammar-school, when he was sixteen or so he proceeded to Paris, where he would have followed the arts course (1135/6–1138). It was the first period of greatness of the Paris schools. Abelard and Peter Lombard were teaching there, and the Englishman Robert of Melun. John of Salisbury, an almost exact contemporary of Thomas, began his studies there in 1136. But of his life and friendships there neither he nor his biographers say a word.

When Thomas was twenty-one his mother, hitherto the greatest influence on his life and conduct, died. It was she who had insisted on his studies and had appreciated his gifts, when Thomas himself was less interested in learning than in field-sports. Now he was free from her insistence, and it was probably at this juncture that he came to know Richer de l'Aigle, a frequent guest in his father's house.[1] Richer, a wealthy baron and Lord of Pevensey castle, was clearly attracted by the handsome, capable and adaptable boy, and initiated him into the lore of hunting with hawks and hounds, the staple occupation of the baronial class when not occupied with military or curial service of any kind. Biographers, contemporary and modern, have pointed out

1. For Richer (d. 1176) see *GW.*, p. 219. He witnessed at Clarendon, *MB.*, iv. 207.

that barriers of class were not at that time as significant as they became later, and that the leading citizens of London in particular were regarded as barons rather than as burgesses.[1] There were, indeed, in the latter part of the twelfth century many instances of a two-way traffic between city and country that has never wholly ceased; landed barons had property and interests in London, and rich citizens bought lands in Hertfordshire and Essex.[2] Thomas, it would seem, spent much time with Richer at Pevensey and elsewhere, and thus picked up the sports and interests of the higher levels of Anglo-Norman society. He had none of John of Salisbury's interest in philosophy or theology; Paris had given him only a fair knowledge of Latin classical literature and a skill in debate and pleading.

Besides being Richer's *protégé* he was also, so one biographer tells us, his notary or confidential secretary, and with him made acquaintance with the royal court, in Stephen's restless days. But this life was cut short by a turn in his father's fortunes. Gilbert fell on evil days, partly owing to loss of property in city fires, and Thomas had to make a living for himself. He, therefore, took service with a friend of his father, Osbern Huitdeniers, as accountant, and either in this capacity or concurrently with it acted as clerk and auditor to the sheriffs of London.[3] He, thus, became acquainted with the methods and policies and interests of the highest levels of mercantile and civic finance, including the collection and accounting of the 'farm' of London, that is, the money raised by the sheriffs to pay the annual sum which the king had established as a condition of freedom for the commune from the exactions of a royal sheriff. In this employment he would also have made acquaintance with the working of the royal exchequer, which was then in process of a reform which ultimately brought it to a condition of high efficiency.

1. W. FitzStephen, *MB.*, iii. 4.
2. This is well illustrated by G. A. Williams, *Medieval London*, London 1963. Williams is chiefly concerned with the thirteenth century, but he also looks backward. See also F. M. Stenton, *Norman London*, 2 ed., 1934 (Historical Association).
3. E. Grim, *MB.*, ii. 361; W. FitzStephen, *MB.*, iii. 14. Osbern was justiciar of London, *c.* 1139–41, while Thomas was his clerk. See J. H. Round, *Geoffrey de Mandeville*, London 1892, 374–5, and *Regesta Regum Anglo-Normannorum*, iii. (edd. Cronne and Davis, Oxford 1968), p. xxv. He was called Huitdeniers ('Eightpence').

In addition, he would have been conversant with the intrigues and negotiations between the Londoners and the various political powers—Stephen, Matilda and the papal legates—in the disturbances and changes of the time. Thomas thus added a knowledge of the world of politics and diplomacy and finance to his previous attainments of a normally educated man conversant with the interests and manners of the court circle.

The next change in Thomas's life came after three years in the City. His personality and efficiency had clearly made their mark, but there is some apparent confusion among his biographers as to how he came to be introduced into the household of the archbishop of Canterbury, the sometime abbot of Bec, Theobald. William FitzStephen, who often carries conviction by his detailed information and obvious human interest, says that two brothers from Boulogne, Baldwin the archdeacon of Sudbury, and Master Eustace, suggested his name.[1] Like Richer, they were often guests at his father's house, and they were also friends of Theobald, but the biographer adds that Thomas's father often reminded the archbishop that they were natives of the same locality and related in some way. Another account, found in two sources,[2] attributes the introduction to an official of Theobald's household who, like the others, was in the habit of staying with Gilbert Becket. Both agencies may have had their share, and in each case Thomas's father was a prime agent in his son's advancement. In the final move, a direct application to the archbishop for a post in his household, Thomas would seem to have acted alone, and the meeting was at Harrow, which had for long been a peculiar of the archbishops of Canterbury.[3] How far his move was due to a natural ambition to air his talents, and how much to a desire for an ecclesiastical rather than an administrative career we do not know. Our answer to the question would depend partly on our opinion of the credibility of the biographers who attribute unusual piety to the boy when he was living at home, and to their account of his resolve to live a life of chastity.[4] The date of his arrival in Theobald's household was probably the winter of 1143–4.

1. W. FitzStephen, *MB.*, iii. 15.
2. E. Grim, *MB.*, ii. 361; Anonymous I, *MB.*, iv. 9.
3. W. FitzStephen, *MB.*, iii. 15.
4. John of Salisbury, *MB.*, ii. 303; H. Bosham, *MB.*, iii. 166.

CHAPTER 2

The English Church

In order to understand the career of Thomas Becket as a church-man it is necessary to consider the condition and problems of the Church in England as he and his master Archbishop Theobald saw it in the reign of Stephen. This implies in its turn a considera-tion of the background of their problems, and this, as in all ecclesiastical matters, may take us very far back in the history of the Church. Far back both Theobald and Thomas were ready to look, but there is a difference between their approach and that of a modern historian. While they turned to the past for direct authority to bear upon the present, we as historians seek rather to search the past for an explanation of present actions and predicaments.

From the earliest times the Church had been a society with rules and precepts of its own both moral and institutional. In the first three centuries this society had developed within the Roman empire, indeed, but without any functional relationship to the emperor and the machinery of government. The Church was an autonomous group within the larger area of the Empire. This state of things was changed suddenly and permanently by the conversion of Constantine. He not only removed the disabilities and restrictions which had lain heavily upon the Christian body, but immediately bestowed privileges and authority upon its priesthood, and constituted himself, the all-powerful emperor, as its immediate protector and, in a very real sense, its moderator. He summoned councils, published and sanctioned orthodox teaching and repressed unorthodoxy and religious rebellion. This created, once and for all, the problem of Church and State. Henceforward, for more than two centuries in the eastern and western churches, and for nine centuries more in the east, at first the Emperor and the patriarchs, with Rome as

paramount, and later the Emperor and the patriarch of Constanti-
nople, shared between them the spiritual and the secular authority,
with a no-man's land of doubtful and disputed territory claimed
and occupied at times by each of the parties.

When the west was separated from the east by political and
economic, as well as by cultural, social and religious differences,
the papacy, which had from very early times claimed a peculiar
apostolic authority as the heir and successor of Peter, was left
in the west without even the semblance of a rival; but from the
eighth century onwards the Carolingian kings provided the
possibility of a rival, and when Italy slipped out of the control
of the Byzantine emperor the papacy willy-nilly succeeded to the
temporal as well as the spiritual government of central Italy.
Little more than a century later, Charlemagne, first as monarch
of western Europe and then as emperor, claimed to hold from
God, as another David, the office of protector and governor of
the people of God, appointing bishops and even pronouncing
upon doctrine, leaving to the pope little more than an ultimate
authority over the faith and church discipline. This position,
which was a reflection half of Old Testament, and half of
Byzantine, theory and practice, was revived after an interval
by the Salic and Hohenstaufen German kings, who claimed a
right, which the papacy never formally allowed, to the title and
position of emperor. When the German phase of the empire
developed, Europe was predominantly under what is known
as the feudal system, and this, together with the prevailing
private ownership of churches and control of their incumbents,
led to a state of things in the ninth and tenth centuries that has
been called 'the church in the hands of laymen', in which rural
priests held office under their feudal lord, and bishops were
appointed and invested in their office by their monarch, and the
papacy itself was regarded as an appointee and vassal of the
emperor. The trend of lay control was reversed in the mid-eleventh
century by the reform of the papacy and the contest between
a series of popes and German kings and emperors, which ended,
in the decades around 1100, with the emancipation, though
not with the complete victory of the papacy. This was both
achieved and followed by a reorganization and centralization
of church government which made of the clergy a class rigidly
separate from the lay estate, with extensive rights and privileges,

and a system of discipline and law which ultimately claimed exclusive jurisdiction over all clerics, and considerable control over the laity in spiritual and quasi-spiritual matters.

So far we have been considering the course of events on the continent of Europe. In Anglo-Saxon and Danish England, united as a single kingdom from the reign of Alfred the Great, church affairs had passed through a different development. In the first place, owing to the gap of almost two centuries between the end of Roman rule in Britain and the conversion to Christianity of the invaders, neither the reality nor the tradition of a paramount emperor had ever existed. Next, the conversion of southern and western England had taken the form of an original mission direct from Pope Gregory, and successive waves of Roman influence had continued for more than a century, so that England, while escaping altogether from the collisions of empire and papacy, yet feeling scarcely at all the distant papal authority as immediate, nevertheless had a tradition and sentiment of gratitude and obedience to Rome as the source and protector of the Christian church which was firmer and warmer than that of any other region save for the areas of north-western Europe that had been evangelized by Anglo-Saxon missionaries. When, however, the country had recovered from the Viking and later Danish invasions the papacy was in eclipse and contact was maintained only by individual pilgrims to Rome, by the traditional offering of Peter's Pence and by the occasional journeys of archbishops for the *pallium*.

In consequence, the English Church, though so close to Rome in sentiment and loyalty, had from Alfred's time onwards developed in complete freedom, and had been interwoven into the country's secular life more closely than any other regional church. Neither kings nor bishops had any need to engage in power-politics similar to those of the German kings and the powerful bishops of the empire. The English kings were devout patrons of the church and the bishops were their counsellors and allies. The great council or Witenagemot was made up of nobles and bishops, and it dealt under the king with every kind of business, secular and ecclesiastical. Bishops were appointed at its meetings and matters of church policy were decided there. As no records or descriptions of the procedure of the Witan exist, we cannot say whether the bishops when need arose formed a committee to discuss church matters and advise the king. All that we know is that the Witan made such decisions.

This intermingling of secular and ecclesiastical persons and administration took place also on a lower level, that of the shire court, of which the bishop was co-president with the royal sheriff. Here again we have scanty records to tell us whether church affairs were dealt with in full session, or whether, as seems likely, the bishops dealt with them apart. In any case, this intermingling of secular and church government in Anglo-Saxon history was unique in the Europe of its day. While it resembled other regions in several important respects, such as the wide prevalence of the proprietary Church and the position of the king as overall controller of church affairs, as universal patron and governor-general, there were also significant differences. The papacy claimed nothing of the Church in England save the ultimate safeguarding of the faith and the bestowal of metropolitan dignity and the abiding loyalty of king and people manifested by the free gift of Peter's-pence. There was not, in consequence, the faintest echo of the tension between pope and monarch. The kings never posed as theologians, and only rarely as reformers, and a recent scholar was fully justified in stating that in England 'the alliance between Church and State was probably more intimate than anywhere else in Europe', while adding that the king 'did not deny, or encroach upon, a bishop's ecclesiastical jurisdiction'.[1] It was in many ways an idyllic situation, but it was possible only in a certain set of historical circumstances and at a certain level of institutional and legal imprecision. The situation was to be changed entirely by the papal reform of the mid-eleventh century and the conquest of England by the Normans in 1066.

The king who was crowned at Westminster in 1066 was already experienced in the hard school of war and repression in the duchy of Normandy, which he had brought to order and unity by his own energy and skill. He had secured his position by force of arms; it was by force of arms that he had conquered the resistance of the English, and the feudalism that he established in his new realm rested upon the relationship of a war-lord to his associates, who held land from him with the obligation

1. F. Barlow, *The English Church*, 1000–1066, London 1963, 152–3. This book gives an excellent survey of the pre-Conquest situation.

of serving him in warfare. In addition, both he and they depended for many years upon military force to control revolts and repel invaders. All this, added to the character of the Normans, seen in all its strength in the Conqueror, made it certain that the kingship of William I would be something very different from that of the Anglo-Saxon monarchy as seen in Athelstan, Edgar and Edward the Confessor.

William I was a statesman, and he intended his rule to show a continuity and a resemblance to that of the previous wearers of the crown which he professed to have inherited lawfully. He used the institutions that he found: the Witan, the machinery of taxation and the royal chapel with its writing clerks, and he allowed the courts of shire, borough and hundred to continue their functions even after the feudal system, like a network, had overlaid the old pattern of landowning, and the feudal honorial and manorial courts had absorbed the economic and tenurial business of the country. Nevertheless, his methods of government were from the start more personal and comprehensive than those of Edward the Confessor. The meetings of the Great Council, which continued the Witan, took place as before, but they were now the meetings of the king with his men, who had won the land with him and whose personal interests were closely bound up with feudal loyalty. They were 'the Frenchmen', the owners of the land and the masters of its population. The Church, in the persons of the bishops and most of the abbots of the old monasteries, had its place in the Great Council, and here for many years there was a small proportion of native prelates, but the king showed his power by summoning bishops and abbots from his Norman duchy to fill vacancies, and if his archbishop of Canterbury, Lanfranc, was more powerful in counsel and action than any archbishop since Dunstan, he was, nevertheless, acting throughout as the lieutenant and agent of the Conqueror, and never as the representative of the Church *vis-à-vis* the authority of the king or interests of State.

The policy and practice of the Conqueror in ecclesiastical matters has often been described.[1] It holds few problems, though

1. Most recently by D. C. Douglas in *William the Conqueror*, London 1964; excellently also by Z. N. Brooke, *The English Church and the Papacy*, Cambridge, 1931 and F. M. Stenton in *The Oxford History of England*, ii, 1943.

it represented a phase in English constitutional history which had no precedent, and did not, and could not, recur. Without being aware of it, the Conqueror had throughout his years in Normandy absorbed in large measure the spirit of order and reform that was abroad in the whole of western Europe in the first half of the eleventh century. It showed itself in the birth of new monastic orders, in the movement towards the eremitical life shared and encouraged by St Peter Damian, in the campaign of Damian and his allies against clerical marriage and immorality in general, in the missionary journeys of Adalbert and others, and in the reforms of the emperors, especially Henry III. It was accompanied by the desire to purify the government of the church by eliminating simony and violent elections of bishops, and it swelled gradually into an attack on the lay ownership of churches and the lay and feudal control of elections to bishoprics and the papacy. Beginning with individual monks and reforming monarchs such as Henry II, it ultimately affected the papacy and changed from being the sum of scattered and individual efforts into an all-embracing policy of reform and centralization, of which the purified papacy was the spearhead.

How far the early stages of the so-called 'Gregorian reform' were familiar to the Conqueror we do not know; he certainly had little sympathy for its policy of centralization. But once in control of England he had to reckon with the Church and with its hierarchy of bishops and abbots. Save for a few (and for William fortunate) personal *débâcles*, one of which left Canterbury vacant, it was not possible for him to clear the ground for a fresh plantation as he had been able to do in the secular sphere after Hastings and subsequent rebellions. But he and his archbishop and counsellor Lanfranc were not content with replacing Englishmen with Normans; they aimed at a wholesale reform of the Church and the monastic body. After half-a-century of controversy, historians are still divided as to the degree of reform necessary in the Anglo-Saxon Church.[1] It was certainly not moribund, and monastic fervour and episcopal energy existed

---

1. Older historians followed William of Malmesbury and other post-Conquest writers. The process of rehabilitation, begun by R. R. Darlington, in 'Ecclesiastical Reform in the Late Old English Period', in *EHR.*, li. (1936), 385–428, has been continued by Barlow (cf. p. 14 n. 1 above) and others.

in the diocese of Worcester, if nowhere else, but, on the other hand, disorganization and lack of precise and canonical lines of demarcation were evident. William and Lanfranc were immediately active in removing a number of sees from rural sites to the nearest town—Selsey to Chichester, Sherborne to Sarum, Elmham to Thetford. Then a series of councils was held by Lanfranc; vacant sees and abbeys were filled, usually by Normans appointed by the king with Lanfranc's counsel, and the rudiments of diocesan organization and monastic reform were attained by the importation of able clerks and monks from Normandy and elsewhere on the continent. William was fortunate in the reservoirs of piety and talent that existed, and a number of outstanding bishops and abbots helped to make the Church in England the equal of that of any other country.

At the same time, the Conqueror made it clear that he was master in his own house, and that the Church was part of his care. His was to be a *Landeskirche*, a territorial Church, part indeed of the Church universal, but a part kept separate from others and under the direct control of the king. Centralization upon the papacy was firmly resisted, though respect for the papacy in the spiritual sphere remained. The relationships between Church and king during the Conqueror's reign were indeed unique. William was as devout as a Norman adventurer could be, blameless in his private life and reformist in his attitude to the Church. He had no theories on the relationship of king and Church, and no preoccupation with law and precedent, whether canonical or regal. His approach was entirely pragmatic, based on broad judgements of suitability and decorum. He took bishops and monks as he found them, and hoped to make them function better. He had no doctrinaire wish to subject the Church to lay control; he drew the bishops and abbots into his feudal system because it seemed logical that they should do service for their estates, many of which were, in fact, gifts from past kings, and because he wished them to defend themselves with a group of knights and supply him with fighting-men; but apart from this he hoped that the Church would conduct its own business and flourish.

Meanwhile Lanfranc, while accepting the overall control of the king, as also the virtual exclusion of all disciplinary and administrative control from outside the realm, pursued his own energetic policy of centralization upon Canterbury and the introduction of canonical practice in matters which the continental reform movements had made familiar to him. It has sometimes been said that Lanfranc's mind had never moved forward from the attitude to reform current in the days before he left Italy for the north. This has been challenged by an examination of his life. He visited Rome and was present at the important Lent synod of 1060. But apart from this, it may be that as a Lombard, his youth in the traditionally anti-papal outlook of his native region had formed his mind in a particular mould. However this may be, Professor Z. N. Brooke, surveying the results of early twentieth-century scholarship in the light of his own researches, showed that Lanfranc had studied and put into practice the points of canon law with which the current law books of north-western Europe had made him familiar.[1] This included a certain amount of organization and discipline while coming well short of the advanced Gregorian doctrine on the papal powers and the prohibition of the bestowal by lay lords of spiritual benefices. This set-up worked very well for the two critical decades in which William I had full control of the kingdom. It demanded the intelligent and free co-operation of a king and an archbishop, each of them with a clear policy and a strength of action acceptable to the other. In its peculiar assignment of the realms of God and Caesar it worked well, as had a somewhat similar arrangement in the days of Dunstan. Indeed, we have to look far down the roll of English history to find another period of equal amity and achievement on the part of a king and an archbishop. It rested entirely on good sense and good will, and neither William nor Lanfranc attempted to put the concordat in the set form of a charter. They realized, as those involved in the disputes of the next century kept repeating, that some things are best left unrecorded: *Expressa nocent*.

When William I and Lanfranc were replaced by William II and Anselm the situation was radically changed. A yoke of oxen had been replaced by a wolf and a lamb. William II exploited the Church which his father had reformed, and Anslem gave a direct and personal religious obedience to the papacy instead of a limited and qualified recognition. When challenged, William II entrenched himself in the customs of his father in refusing to

1. Z. N. Brooke, *The English Church and the Papacy*, 57–83.

allow entrance to papal letters and clearance of appeals to Rome. Anselm in exile first learnt at first hand of the papal reforms in the matter of investiture (that is, the bestowal of the insignia of church office by the king and his acceptance of homage before consecration) and insisted on their observance. This led to his second exile and the agreement of 1107, which antedated by fifteen years the more celebrated concordat of Worms. This agreement was at first sight a victory for Anselm. Henry abandoned investiture but retained the right to feudal homage which (contrary to the papal wishes) he exacted in practice before consecration; he retained also in practice the virtual right of appointment, either by disregarding the canonical freedom of election or by holding the election in his chapel where he could control the situation.

Thus by 1107 the position of both parties had changed. William I had taken over the government of a country where the Church was living quietly under a system, or lack of system, of which the roots went back several centuries and which owed its existence to a lack of will and ability on the part of the papacy to interfere in any way with the normal course of church life. He had made of an indefinite way of acting a firm programme of government, stiffening and increasing the bulwarks of independence. His sons in their turn had frozen his supple way of acting into rigid 'customs'. Concurrently, while Lanfranc had concentrated on a reform controlled by himself and implemented by canonical material of his own selection, Anselm held and promulgated the advanced papal claims in their fully developed form. Anselm was succeeded after a long interval by two archbishops of less ability and determination. Henry I, by political dexterity and strength of will, succeeded in maintaining the practice of his father's reign with certain exceptions, such as the abandonment of investiture and the acceptance of papal legates, of whom an archbishop of Canterbury was one. But the ecclesiastical climate of western Europe had changed and was still rapidly changing outside and independent of the movements of English politics.

The emergence of Europe from childhood into adolescence in the eleventh century began with a revival of the regular religious life, and continued with a campaign against widespread abuses in Church and society, such as clerical marriage and incontinence, gross immorality in towns, simony in elections of all kinds and excessive wealth among prelates. The latter part of the century saw the rise of new monastic orders and a revival of the institute of regular canons, and finally in the birth of the Cistercian order with its wide appeal to the illiterate as well as to the educated levels of society. The Cistercians, soon followed and imitated by the white or Norbertine canons, enjoyed a vogue without parallel in western and central Europe, and taken together with the continued growth of the traditional black monks, brought into the consciousness of all countries the dedicated life of monks and canons as a universal ideal, the one certain harbour of salvation. The rise of the new orders was accompanied by the appearance of a galaxy of saints, almost all monks or canons. Peter Damian; John Gualbert and Romuald; Aubrey and Stephen Harding among the first Cistercians, Stephen of Muret, Gilbert of Sempringham, Ailred of Rievaulx, Ivo of Chartres are names taken at random. They could easily be trebled in number, and among the additions would be several of the reforming popes, such as Leo IX, Gregory VII, Urban II and Eugenius III. This emergence of sanctity, and above all that of the prestigious Bernard of Clairvaux, who stood out among his contemporaries as did Napoleon in another age and sphere, displayed to all men the regular life and the new organization of the church as something bearing the stamp of spiritual success and divine guidance. Moreover, as all these new institutes looked to the papacy for approval and protection, and were the recipients of its commendation and favour, they became everywhere links of the chain that bound the regional churches more closely to Rome, and supported the papal policy as mirrored in the solemn councils that took place at the Lateran and elsewhere under the presidency of the popes of the new model. Appeal to Rome, that had fallen into desuetude for centuries save in cases of extreme importance, was now accepted as normal, and disputes of all kinds, with the inevitable traffic to and from Rome were decided in the Curia or, from the mid-twelfth century onwards, entrusted to local judges-delegate.

To the purely religious revival must be added the literary, intellectual and educational upsurge, which was the work almost exclusively of monks and clerics. This in north-western Europe attracted able and ambitious young people to Paris, to Chartres, to Laon and elsewhere, and to the individual teachers such as

Berengarius, Roscelin, Lanfranc and Abelard, and later to the nascent university of Paris. The literary and dialectical training, again almost entirely the province of clerks, made possible the great wave of controversial and propagandist literature, and concentrated many of the best minds of Europe upon the business of the church. This fervent new life, which made of the century between 1050 and 1150 one of the germinal and fruitful epochs of European history, must be held in every historian's and every reader's mind as the background of all the achievements and combats of the age. The phrase 'age of faith' is used too loosely and with limits too wide for accuracy of all the centuries of the middle ages. It is an apt description of the early twelfth century above all. Despite the ignorance, license and brutality of the age, belief in God and in the Church of God permeated every class of society in a way that it had not done in the earlier centuries and did no longer from the end of the thirteenth century onwards. The clearest evidence of this comes from the classes of the baronage, of the royal administration, and of royalty itself. All these men, in the main, whatever their personal morals or pursuits, recognized in the last instance the existence of a re-warding and avenging God, and of the validity of spiritual commands and sanctions, and the worth of spiritual ideals. Both Henry II and Henry VIII were selfish, obstinate and faithless in human relationships, and both used the language of piety. But whereas to Henry VIII the law and the will of God are indistinguishable from his own, Henry II, with whatever bad grace and bad faith, recognized the law of God and of the Church as existing independently of what he himself might desire, and as having authority.

CHAPTER 3

Theobald's Clerk

WILLIAM STUBBS, in a phrase that has become hackneyed, described the household of the archbishop of Canterbury in Theobald's day as 'to some extent' satisfying 'the want which was afterwards met by the university system'.[1] The great historian was careful to qualify his judgment, and, writing before English scholars were familiar with the intellectual life of Europe, may be excused for leaving the existing schools of Paris, Chartres, Laon and the rest out of his reckoning, but a collection of ten or twelve career ecclesiastics, however individually brilliant, does not satisfy any educational want. A better comparison might, perhaps, have been made with All Souls College at Oxford. Nevertheless, a group of men that contained John of Salisbury and Vacarius the lawyer, together with half-a-dozen future bishops and archbishops, did not lack distinction, and the atmosphere into which the young Thomas of London was introduced must have been very stimulating, the more so as Theobald and his officers and advisers were engaged in a struggle for power against the king and his able group of clerks, and could feel that great events and a great cause depended upon their efforts and skill.

Nor must we forget that the archbishop's *familia* lived in the same complex of great buildings as did the monks of the cathedral priory. This community, in the mid-twelfth century, was the largest and one of the most distinguished in the country. The presence of monks as the choral staff and chapter of a cathedral was a peculiarly English institution, dating from the monastic reform of the tenth century, when King Edgar and his archbishop Dunstan and bishops Ethelwold and Oswald used monks as agents of a general reform of clerical life in the country. Whether

1. W. Stubbs, *Seventeen Lectures on the Study of Medieval and Modern History*, London 1886, 142.

Canterbury cathedral, as distinct from St Augustine's abbey, contained a community of monks from the days of Augustine has long been a matter of controversy, but it would seem at least highly probable that Dunstan introduced (or reintroduced) monastic life to Christ Church, though he may, like Oswald at Worcester, have done so by stages and incompletely. A quasi-monastic life was in existence in 1066, but the influence of archbishop Stigand, the nominal abbot, after 1052 must have been discouraging. In any case, the house was reformed thoroughly by Lanfranc, who fully accepted his position as abbot. He introduced a prior from Bec and a number of other Norman monks, and gave them a complete monastic and liturgical directory based on those of the most observant continental houses. It is always dangerous, without further evidence, to argue that a religious house keeps its way of life faithfully, but the character of Lanfranc and of his monastic successor Anselm, together with the writings of Eadmer, Anselm's confidant, suggests that a very high level of monastic observance prevailed there during the first forty years after the Conquest, and probably until the vexatious and demoralising controversies at the end of the twelfth century. During most of this period it was the largest monastery of black monks in England, with up to 150 in the community c.1125. Some of Anselm's theological writings and letters were composed for his monks, and Eadmer's Life and other writings are evidence of the level of learning attained at Christ Church. Its library by 1150 was probably the largest in the country, and Canterbury was also a centre of illumination. Between 1130 and 1180 some of the finest examples of a distinguished period of artistic achievement were executed in its cloister. Among the masterpieces was the celebrated 'Lambeth' Bible, one of the supreme works of the English middle ages; the whole school has been studied fully by Professors Wormald and Dodwell.[1] Alongside the artists in the scriptorium, were the scribes, and here again Canterbury, helped by émigrés from Bec, was a centre of exact and beautiful writing.

Besides the cathedral monastery there was at Canterbury and within a few hundred yards of the cathedral the large church and monastery of St Augustine's, the jealous rival of Christ

1. Especially C. R. Dodwell, *The Canterbury School of Illumination*, Cambridge 1954.

Church, claiming Augustine as its founder and patron and holding his tomb and those of many of his successors. Though an unruly house in Lanfranc's day, probably owing to an element of Anglo-Saxon disaffection in the community, and soon troubled with the long controversy over exemption with the archbishop, St Augustine's was yet another home of art and learning, and it is in this sense, as the focus of three different centres of mental activity, that Canterbury in the twelfth century had some likeness to a university city in a later age. Thus the archbishop's household, itself almost a religious house in its practices and discipline, lived and worked in surroundings different from almost all the other cathedrals of England. Westminster, and the new centre of teaching at Oxford, were perhaps the only places with a similar variety of mental interest. The accounts of the archbishop's life at Canterbury, including the narratives of his last day, show how close the intercourse was with some, at least, of the monks, and from the monastic chroniclers we can see that their knowledge of what went on in the archbishop's household was accurate. Canterbury, when Thomas of London arrived there, must have been a stimulating place. Through it passed the majority of travellers to and from the continent, in addition to the archbishop's messengers coming and going, and in another field of interest there can have been few years when there were no new constructions in train at one or the other of the two great churches. The air at midnight and sunrise must have been full of the sound of bells great and small, while the lanes echoed to the hooves of the horses coming to the courts of the two monasteries and the stables of the archbishop.

When he joined the household of Theobald at Canterbury, Thomas was twenty-five years old and in the bloom of young manhood. We have more than one description of his appearance.[1] He was tall, gracefully built, and dark-haired, with an aquiline nose and pale complexion which showed a flush when he was excited. All his senses of sight, hearing, taste and smell were abnormally keen, and he had a remarkably tenacious and exact memory. This last quality may be borne in mind when we meet with unexpected silences and inaccuracies in some of his utterances. His mind moved rapidly, and he could as rapidly find words

1. E. Grim, *MB.*, ii. 359–60; W. FitzStephen, *MB.*, iii. 17; *Thómas Saga*, RS. i. 29.

for his thoughts; he was redoubtable in argument and repartee. With our knowledge of his later history we are at first surprised to learn that he sought to please others by falling in with their ways of life and pursuits, and by making himself agreeable to all, but it is probable that those who attribute these qualities to him are thinking mainly or solely of his early years. To these years also belong the charges of human respect, extravagance, display and ambition; but his many biographers, including his companions of many years and his confessor, agree that he was in all things a lover of truth and absolutely chaste. At the time of his service in Theobald's household he was undoubtedly set upon making a career for himself among those who were for the most part more highly born, yet the statement of one biographer that his parents dedicated him to the priesthood in infancy may well have been true. It would explain his readiness to leave the City for Canterbury, and also his father's eagerness to help him in this.

Very little is known of the personal activities of Theobald's *familia* at this time save what is told by the biographers of Thomas. Roger of Pont l'Evêque and John of Canterbury were among the clerks on the staff on his arrival, the one to become his inveterate opponent, the other a faithful ally when the former was archbishop of York and the latter bishop of Poitiers. Walter, brother of the archbishop and later bishop of Rochester, was archdeacon of Canterbury. Thomas, Roger and John were for a time associated in a pact of mutual assistance in the picking up of preferment, but the relations of Roger and Thomas were often strained. Roger, the elder, apparently envious of the 'new boy's' success with Theobald, treated him as an inferior and gave him the name of 'the clerk with the hatchet', a reference to the surname, Baille-Hache, of the official who had introduced him to Theobald, and perhaps an allusion to Thomas's energy in clearing his way to promotion. He even succeeded in having him twice unfairly dismissed from the archbishop's service. On each occasion he was sheltered by Walter the archdeacon until the charge against him had been dismissed.[1]

1. William of Canterbury, *MB.*, i. 4; W. FitzStephen, *MB.*, iii. 16. Theobald's marshal, Baillehache, who brought Thomas to Theobald, and inspired Roger's nickname for Thomas, witnesses one of the archbishop's charters, see A. Saltman, *Theobald, Archbishop of Canterbury*, London 1956, no. 255, p. 482.

To enter Theobald's household was not for Thomas merely a move from one office to another. He left a purely secular establishment for a society concerned directly with the Church. Although the group of clerks may have been restless and ambitious, they had embarked on a career of which the spiritual element might be obscured, but could not be wholly neglected in the prevailing atmosphere of the twelfth century. Moreover, Theobald was a monk and according to all evidence a man of sincere piety and observance. As archbishop he stood *in loco abbatis* to the community of Christ Church and as ex-abbot of Bec could scarcely forget his two great predecessors of abbatial rank. We do not know how closely he conformed to the practice of Lanfranc and Anselm thirty years earlier, and to the spirit of Lanfranc's constitutions, but it is to be supposed that routine in his hall and some of the daily exercises of his household were based on the monastic regime, for we know what the daily life of the group was when Thomas became archbishop, and it is scarcely likely that Thomas would have instituted a way of life for his clerks that was notably more severe than that which he had experienced himself. The accounts of his external change of life from that of a young man on the fringe of court society to that of a serious-minded young cleric are, therefore, probably true in substance.

There is no direct record of Thomas's duties as archbishop's clerk. His life, apart from its religious duties, must have resembled, with all reserves of time and place, that of a promising young man in a Ministry who is acting as personal private secretary to a Minister. He would have seen how the machine worked and how Theobald guided it. He would have seen how the archbishop beat off royal encroachments or played his cards in the ceaseless political broils of the day, somewhat as the young man in the Ministry shares in the plans and anxieties of his chief when Bills are being torn to pieces in the House or threats of a general election are blighting his hopes. There were some, at least, of Theobald's letters to write. John of Salisbury did not arrive for several years and in any case much of the routine correspondence must have fallen to juniors. There were the rents of the estates of the archbishop to deal with, and the house property to oversee. How many of the household remained at Canterbury when Theobald went the round of his manors, or up to Lambeth, or to meetings of the Great Council at Woodstock

or Clarendon we do not know, but the biographers suggest
that this young man, attractive as a companion and eager to
please, energetic also and efficient, was picked out from the first
by Theobald as his confidant. If so, he would have moved about
with his patron. In 1148, as he himself related some years later,[1]
he was the sole companion of the archbishop when Theobald,
forbidden to obey the pope's summons to a Council at Rheims,
escaped by night from England in a skiff manned by two unskilled
boatmen—an exhibition, as Pope Eugenius remarked, of swimming
rather than of sailing.[2] On several other occasions he made the
journey to Rome, the first being with Theobald who went there
in some state, and if the visit of March 1144 be this, he was
accompanied by the bishops of Ely and Coventry, and the
advocacy of Thomas was rewarded by the benefice of Otford.[3]
He is said also to have been mainly responsible, as Theobald's
agent, for the final papal refusal by Eugenius III in 1152 of
Stephen's proposal to crown his son Eustace as heir to the
throne.[4] Eustace in the event died in 1153, but the decision of
Eugenius left, and was intended to leave, the validity of Stephen's
title to the crown of England questionable; hence Thomas was
indirectly making the candidature of Prince Henry viable. At
some time also, though unfortunately no date is specified, Thomas
was sent by Theobald to study civil and canon law at Bologna
and Auxerre. As to his studies, his masters and his acquaintance-
ships, we are completely in the dark, as we are with other of his
contemporaries, such as Gilbert Foliot. The decades 1140–1160
were crucial in the history of intellectual life in Europe, for
between those dates appeared various editions and recensions
of the two text-books that were to form the basis of all instruction
of canon law and theology in the schools for the next three
centuries: the *Concordia discordantium canonum* of Gratian, and
the *Sentences* of Peter Lombard, the one a monk of Bologna,
the other a secular master (later bishop) of Paris. Gratian's
great work was probably completed about 1140, some years

1. Archbishop Thomas to Cardinal Boso, *MB.*, vi. (250), 57–8.
2. *MB.*, vi. 58. 'Natando potius quam navigando'.
3. W. FitzStephen, *MB.*, iii. 17. For his journey, see *GFL.*, 505–6.
4. The only authority is Gervase, *Chronicle*, i. 150 (cf. *TL.*, 45). Cf.*MB.*,
vi. (250), 58, and Kate Norgate in the *D.N.B.*

before Thomas was at Bologna. Among the celebrated masters
of that centre of legal studies was Rolando Bandinelli, the future
Pope Alexander III. He had probably left for a curial appointment before Thomas arrived, but his name would have been
remembered with respect.

The purpose of Thomas's *Studienjahr* was doubtless to prepare
him for an administrative post such as the archdeaconry, for
which Theobald may have been grooming him betimes. If so,
he would have given his attention to procedural law rather than
to theories of church and state, or theology. We know very little
of Thomas's career between this and his first great promotion.
Life at Canterbury must have been made more exhilarating by
the arrival of John of Salisbury in 1147. Nothing is known of
his relations with Thomas till events parted them and gave us
John's letters, but it is clear that friendship of a certain degree
of warmth grew up between them. How warm and intimate this
was is very hard to say, and all modern biographers of Thomas
and John would give much for certain information. Thomas
had few if any intimate friends, and John's sincere admiration
and loyalty in later years are unquestionable, as are Thomas's
trust in John and esteem of his counsel. But attitudes such as
these do not necessarily imply the warmth and easy give and take
of affectionate friendship between equals, and of this there is
no clear evidence, possibly because we know so little of Thomas's
intimate relations with those around him. Nor can we say precisely
what the dedication by John to Thomas of the *Policraticus* and
Metalogicon may imply.

In 1154, on Theobald's recommendation, Roger of Pont
l'Evêque was elected archbishop of York, and consecrated a
few days before King Stephen's death (10 and 25 October).
Thomas was immediately appointed to the vacant archdeaconry
of Canterbury and provostship of Beverley; the archdeaconry
was perhaps the most important ecclesiastical position in England
below the episcopal level. He was not, however, permitted to
show his abilities in a life committed to diocesan administration.
Only a few weeks afterwards, again on the recommendation of
Theobald supported by Henry of Winchester, Philip bishop of
Bayeux, and Arnulf, bishop of Lisieux, the new king appointed
him his chancellor. Theobald's aim was undoubtedly to secure
a fair deal for the Church in the new reign, in which he foresaw

a reaction from the loose and inconsistent government of Stephen. It is interesting to note that Theobald's foresight in 1154 was at fault in his estimate of Thomas; Henry was equally at fault eight years later.

The exact date of Thomas's appointment is not known, but there is evidence that it was very early in the reign, at latest in January 1155, more probably at the Christmas council of December 1154.[1] Many years later, in his final letter of accusation to the archbishop, Gilbert Foliot accused Thomas of buying office with the bid of an unspecified but considerable sum of money.[2] There are certainly instances throughout the twelfth century of a price being paid, or even exacted, for high posts in the royal service, and we cannot be sure that Thomas, at this stage of his career, would have boggled at such a transaction. But as there is clear evidence that his candidature was strongly supported and that Henry made his decision rapidly and willingly, we may conclude that if money passed it was at the king's formal or tacit request, not as a bid or a bribe; but there are many inaccurate and unproved defamatory suggestions in Foliot's letter, and his charge, in default of corroboration, must be considered unproven.

Indeed, the course of events would seem to eliminate the probability of deliberate negotiations on Thomas's part. Henry had been out of the country for more than six months when Stephen died (25 October) and he did not return to England before 8 December. He was crowned king on 19 December and held an important council at his Christmas crown-wearing when, as we have seen, Thomas's appointment may have taken place. The biographers are clear and in agreement that the principal advocate was Theobald, and that his motives were, first and foremost, to protect the interests of the Church against the king's servants, the 'wild beasts at court',[3] and, secondly, to act with reason and humanity in the drive to restore order and

---

1. So *TL.*, 55–7, with full references.
2. *MB.*, v. (225), 523–4; *GFL.*, no. 170. This point also is discussed carefully in *TL.*, 62–4.
3. The phrase is from John of Salisbury: 'pugnare ad bestias curiae' (*MB.*,i i. 305). Herbert of Bosham prefers 'aulicorum vermis' [i.e. serpent] (*MB.*, iii. 177). William of Canterbury has John's phrase (*MB.*, i. 5).

the king's government in the land. Unless we suppose that Henry discussed his future appointments with Theobald and others a year or more before Stephen's death, there can have been little time for manoeuvring between Henry's return and the probable date of Thomas's entry into office.

CHAPTER 4

The Chancellor

(i) The Chancellor and the Kingdom

WHEN Henry of Anjou became king the machinery of government needed an almost complete overhaul. The rule of William I after the Conquest was all but entirely personal. The king, who consulted his tenants-in-chief three or four times a year in meetings that replaced those of the Anglo-Saxon Witan, carried out his policy through individuals, both churchmen such as his brother Odo, bishop of Bayeux, and Lanfranc, or leading barons. In the country as a whole the king was represented by his sheriff in each country, and by the marcher lords on the borders of Wales. Gradually a smaller council came into being, consisting of some barons and bishops who were habitually used by the king. When the king went abroad an individual was deputed to take his place: Odo of Bayeux at first, and Lanfranc later, acted in this way. They and other barons considered such great pleas or trials as might arise. The practice of William II was similar, but now with Ranulf Flambard appeared the type of the efficient parvenu rising to the top by reason of his success in meeting the king's need for money and for tolerably smooth administration. Henry I for a long time used his wife and later his son as regents, but when both were dead he turned to Roger, bishop of Salisbury. Roger, like Ranulf, had risen by reason of his great administrative talents, and his bishopric was the reward of service. He is significant as being the creator of what may be anachronistically called the civil service. His official position was that of justiciar, and in this he may be said to have founded the exchequer as an instrument of government, and to have rationalized its business.

The medieval chancellor, who took his name from the lattice behind which the minor Roman official originally did his work, was in origin the head of the royal chapel, that is, the ensemble of relics, books, furniture and clerks which followed the court wherever it went. He, aided by one or more clerks, executed most of the royal writs, letters and charters, and authenticated them all with the royal seal of which he had custody. As is well known, all the organs of medieval English government developed from the activities of the king's household, and of this the chapel was an important part. Another member was the treasurer, and when the financial business increased the treasurer's department was amalgamated with a part of the chancellor's activities and became the exchequer. This was in origin the office of receipt into which was delivered the 'farm', or monetary contribution to government, of the various shires collected by the respective sheriffs, and any rates and dues not included in the farm. Though the treasurer was the official president, the chancellor, as keeper of the royal seal, was an essential member of the court and alone could issue payments and receipts. Gradually, therefore, his activities and staff expanded, while the treasurer remained principally as custodian and disburser of the king's moneys. Roger of Salisbury, who introduced the abacus, a method of reckoning with counters on a cloth ruled like a chessboard, recruited three of his young relations and ran the administration as a family group. His nephew became chancellor, a second nephew, Nigel, treasurer and bishop of Ely, while another relative, Alexander, bishop of Lincoln, was his ally.

Henry I, a strong king, built up a group of servants partly from the feudal ranks and partly 'from the dust'; they joined Roger and his relatives at the exchequer and served as royal agents and justices, for there was as yet no professional judiciary. The old English courts of hundred (or borough) and shire still functioned, and the latter under the sheriff retained its importance, but the most important pleas came before the Curia Regis, which was a court of first instance for tenants-in-chief and a court of appeal from itinerant justices when these began to function in Henry I's reign. The Curia Regis was composed of the royal household officials and a few other barons. The barons of the exchequer, who were often called upon to adjudicate in matters of payment and went on circuit to assess revenues, were often used by the king to try pleas as members of the Curia.

The history and functions of the exchequer as a financial office have been narrated often and well with the aid of the remarkable

and full *Dialogue of the Exchequer* written by one of its officials
in the latter part of the reign of Henry II.[1] The great future which
lay before the office and the title of chancellor of the exchequer
borne by one of its members (who was in origin a Treasurer's
clerk, not the Chancellor himself) has led to a common belief
that the exchequer was the chancellor's main sphere of activity.
In fact, he seems to have been present but rarely, and for Thomas
it was certainly only a small part of his life. As his early training
had been financial, he was no doubt perfectly at ease when
present, and his remarkable memory would have enabled him
to remain *au courant* with its work, but it was not precisely as
chief of the chancery or the exchequer that he deployed his gifts.
He lifted his title of office momentarily to princely eminence
not only and perhaps not chiefly by his work at the exchequer,
but by his achievements and conduct as *alter ego* to the king.
This phase of his career has been treated only cursorily by
historians. Those interested in secular matters find in it little
of the great work of legal and institutional reform that made
the later decades of the reign so remarkable, and church historians
concentrate their interest upon the career of Thomas as archbishop. Yet for a knowledge of Thomas's character and abilities
these years are very revealing. Setting aside for the moment all
spiritual considerations, we may consider the courage, the
decision, and the swift efficiency of the newly-appointed archdeacon of Canterbury in his still more recent office. Without
the advantage of birth in the baronage or of a *pied-à-terre* in
the form of lands or feudal connections to strengthen his hand
and his resolve, without the training in the court and exchequer
possessed by his subordinates, Thomas entered upon his office
as master of the king's chapel and writing-office by organizing,
if not actually leading, those occupied in 'slighting' the adulterine
castles of the most powerful barons, including those of the
ex-legate and king-maker Henry of Winchester, to whose advocacy
he stood beholden. The eight years of his chancellorship, indeed,
are all but unique in the annals of the English monarchy between
the Conquest and the days of Wolsey. At no other time did a
minister of the Crown combine the assets of complete royal
confidence and delegation of power with such talents of

1. The latest and best edition is by C. Johnson, *Dialogus de Scaccario*,
London 1950, (Nelson's Medieval Texts), with excellent introduction.

administration, of diplomacy and of display. When Thomas became chancellor he was almost exactly thirty-six, while the king was twenty-one. But it was not by age or past experience that he secured his ascendancy. Henry had had his full share of experience in war and diplomacy; he had already added to his dominions by bold action and by the swift appropriation of his rival Louis's discarded but lavishly gifted and fiercely energetic wife Eleanor. But the young king was high-spirited, buoyant, extroverted, and emotional, and Thomas, equally extroverted, always disposed to take his colour from his surroundings, and with no one else to claim his personal devotion, was drawn to his king by both a genuine quasi-elder brother affection, and by the glamour of royalty and court life.

It is difficult to give a connected account of Thomas's activities in the years of his chancellorship. With the exception of Fitz-Stephen the biographers pass rapidly over this period of his life and give a general picture of his relationship with the king rather than a narrative with a series of events in chronological order. This relationship was, indeed, a fact of the greatest significance in Thomas's life. His actions, thoughts and fortunes, were for the sixteen years of his life in high office, so entwined with those of his king, and each was so influenced by the other on the personal, emotional level, that the historian of Thomas must make some attempt to comprehend the character and personality of Henry II.

For such a study the information appears at first sight to be ample. In addition to the king's actions and *acta*, and the many good narrative sources for his policies and reaction to events, there are numerous descriptions of his character. The age was one in which intelligent men examined the outstanding personalities of their time with a sensitivity and a sympathy unknown to any other century of the middle ages. We have only to think of the biographers of Bernard, of Ailred, of Samson of Bury, and of Thomas himself to realize this, and John of Salisbury in his writings and letters gives us pen-pictures of the great men he had known that are unsurpassed in their *finesse* and in their balance. Of Henry himself we have half-a-dozen or more set pieces of characterisation, which both supplement and corroborate each other.

Despite this, Henry remains something of an enigma, partly

because he drew from different men phrases of excessive admiration and hostility, partly because his character and qualities of mind were complex and unusual, and are seen by us against an unfamiliar, almost incomprehensible, background of feeling and thought. One thing at least is clear, that Henry was no ordinary mortal. Those who knew him felt his distinction, and would have agreed with Walter Map, who knew him well, that he was 'one upon whom men gazed closely a thousand times, yet took occasion to return,[1] and with Gerald of Wales, who likewise knew the king intimately, that had he conquered his faults of character 'he would have been beyond comparison among the princes of this world for his many natural gifts',[2] and with John of Salisbury, who, as we shall see, could on occasion be scathing in his criticism of Henry, but who, even at the height of the great quarrel, could use almost the same words as Gerald, that if only Henry could control himself and show due reverence for the Church 'he has such remarkable gifts of nature and grace (!), that no prince, I would think, or certainly very few princes, as I would say without hesitation, is his equal.'[3] Finally, there is the long and celebrated description of Henry and his character by Peter of Blois.[4] Certainly, in attempting to recreate his personality, we must make allowance not only for human failings, for the bias of those opposed to his policies, and for the medieval animus against authority, but the difficulty still remains that some of the most carefully framed judgments of contemporaries conflict with their own and others' descriptions of the king's behaviour.

1. W. Map, *De Nugis Curialium*, ed. M. R. James in *Anecdota Oxoniensia*, Medieval and Modern Series, xiv. (1914), 237–42. English translation in *EHD.*, ii. (17).
2. Giraldus Cambrensis, *Opera Omnia*, RS., v. 302–6; viii. 155–75, 282–97, 304–6. English translation in *EHD.*, ii. (15, 16). The words in the text are on p. 388.
3. *MB.*, vi. (457), 500.
4. Peter of Blois, *Ep.* 66, printed in *MB.*, vii. (800), 570–6. This galaxy of encomia, set side by side with the eulogies of St Thomas, provide a 'headache for historians'. Peter of Blois, indeed, solves the difficulty by carrying straight on with praise of the martyr, the 'special patron' of the king who, Peter swears, was entirely innocent of the murder. As for Gerald and Map, they provide elsewhere plenty of ammunition to destroy their own constructions.

All agree that life at his court was strenuous to a degree. He was incessantly on the move from crack of dawn till evening, and even then tired his companions out by refusing to sit down. Moreover, his decisions to move, and the direction of his movements, were made to all appearances on the spur of the moment. 'He moved in intolerably long stages, like a special courier, and showed no mercy to his companions'.[1] He was always active and extrovert, discussing and issuing orders even at Mass, yet there was nothing in him of the restlessness of the neurotic. All agree that his fits of rage could be formidable and ungovernable, yet all agree also that he was 'exceedingly good and lovable and that no one 'surpassed him in gentleness and friendliness'.[2] Unperturbed and affable in the midst of a demanding crowd, he was 'easy of access and condescending, pliant and witty, second to none in politeness'.[3] That these qualities are not the invention of courtiers we can see from incidents such as that related by St Hugh of Lincoln. The Charterhouse of Witham housed a lay-brother well known for his freedom of speech. This man on one occasion took the king to task for his failure to provide for his foundation at Witham with such fierceness that Hugh, himself no great respecter of persons, could never recall the incident without a feeling of acute discomfort.[4] Yet Henry took the rebuke without anger and bore no malice. Mention of Hugh may remind us that Henry respected, and was respected by, three other saints besides Thomas. Hugh the Carthusian, whom he made bishop of Lincoln, he loved in later life so dearly that it was rumoured that the monk was his son. Ailred of Rievaulx dedicated two of his works to him and gave him counsel,[5] and Henry was one of those who wrote to the pope on behalf of Gilbert of Sempringham when he was the object of calumny to the lay-brothers of his order.[6]

1. W. Map, p. 237; cf. *EHD.*, ii. 389.
2. *EHD.*, ii. 390.
3. Giraldus Cambrensis, *EHD.*, ii. 386.
4. *Magna Vita Sancti Hugonis*, ed. D. Douie and H. Farmer, London 1961–2, i. 66. (Nelson's Medieval Texts).
5. The works were the *Genealogia Regum Anglorum* and the *Life* of Edward the Confessor. Ailred is said to have advised the king to acknowledge Alexander III.
6. Knowles, 'The Revolt of the Lay Brothers of Sempringham', in *EHR.*, l. (1935).

A similar mixture of qualities is seen in his political and diplomatic actions. He could be swift in movement to seize a momentary chance, as in his adolescence when he brought off the remarkable *coup* of marriage with Eleanor of Aquitaine, yet Map notices as one of his faults the interminable delays with which he put off his suitors and claimants.[1] Though he was neither by temperament nor design a lawgiver, and made few if any original additions to legal procedure, his reorganization and regularization of the judicial eyre, the use of the local jury in the possessory and other assizes, the extension of the jurisdiction of the royal courts by means of the possessory writs, and the reissue and development of old unwritten customs and new issues in the Constitutions of Clarendon and the Assizes of Clarendon and Northampton, though all were probably adopted primarily as a means of strengthening the royal control of the country and increasing the revenue of the Crown, were in fact part of the policy of a clear-sighted man who wished to eliminate feuds and self-help, to create an atmosphere of stability, and to collect all the reins of power into the hands of a central, professional group of officials. We are not here concerned chiefly with assessing Henry's work as a great sovereign or assessing the part played by subordinates, but it is on every count remarkable that a monarch with dominions spread so widely, and with diplomatic and dynastic connections widespread over Europe, should have exerted such a potent influence over the government and development of the country which he visited comparatively rarely, and should have inspired trust in so many scattered groups of officials.

Gerald of Wales observed that 'whom he had once hated he scarcely ever loved' subsequently, 'but whom he had once loved he scarcely ever called to mind with hatred'.[2] His relationship with Thomas Becket provides a commentary upon these words, and we have to decide whether to declare Gerald in error, or to suppose that the king's long war with the archbishop was an endeavour to hurt one whom he had never truly loved and who would not put devotion to the king above all other interests. When all is said, Henry eludes judgement. Few who consider his character can avoid making a mental comparison with Henry

1. W. Map, *EHD.*, ii. 390.
2. Giraldus Cambrensis, *EHD.*, ii. 387. Peter of Blois apparently anticipates Giraldus in *MB.*, vii. (800), 573.

VIII; there is a deceptively similar mixture of great abilities, capacity to evoke loyal service and admiration, lasting achievement, grave character faults and ultimate failure to realize what youth had promised. Yet the differences are as great as the resemblances. Henry II lacked the all-absorbing and ultimately destructive egoism of Henry VIII, as also his ruthless treatment of both enemies and devoted servants. Most of Henry II's ministers, with the obvious exception of Thomas, remained undisturbed in his service throughout their lives; there are no savage executions or judicial murders in his reign. We may almost say that he was unjust only when he lost his self-control. In the matter of religion, while Henry VIII, at least from the middle of his reign onwards, was without a semblance of spiritual religion, Henry II, for all his moral lapses and other faults, never lost the sense that God and the Church of Christ were of a higher order of being than his own affairs. Nor did the reign of Henry II show the eclipse of fair sunshine or the failure to use opportunity that is apparent in that of Henry VIII. The crisis of the tragedy of Thomas Becket was not a climacteric point. Henry recovered his poise and some of his most influential legal reforms date from his last years. His later catastrophes were largely due to the selfish and irresponsible behaviour of his sons, though their father cannot be considered wholly blameless.

The king left England in January 1156 to resist his brother's claims to Anjou and Maine, and to receive homage from Aquitaine. A single reference by a chronicler, Gervase of Canterbury, mentions the presence of the chancellor and his great assistance in the campaign.[1] Thomas was not long abroad, for he was acting in several countries as an itinerant justice later in the year.[2] In 1158 Henry was abroad again, and it was in this year that the chancellor led his remarkable embassy from the coast to Paris and conducted the negotiations for the marriage of the infant daughter Margaret of Louis VII with the king's eldest son, securing the Vexin for her dowry. The following year Henry moved south to make good his wife's claim to the countship of Toulouse, actually held by Raymund of St Gilles, now brother-in-law of Louis, who supported him against Henry and occupied

---

1. Gervase, *Chronicle*, i. 162, *s.a.* 1156.
2. For Thomas as justice itinerant see *Pipe Roll 2 Henry* II, pp. 17, 26, 65, 89. He visited at least ten counties.

D

Toulouse. The king moved against the city with Thomas as
organizer and leader of a part of his army. Thomas urged him
to take the city, but Henry shrank from attacking a place occupied
by his feudal lord, the king of France.[1] It was in this campaign
that the chancellor rode at the head of a company of seven
hundred knights raised by himself as well as his own feudal
array, plus an alleged twelve thousand mercenaries. All these
were paid by the scutage and *donum* now levied on all knights'
fees of ecclesiastical as well as of secular baronies.[2] Thomas
himself fought with distinction at the head of his men and
ravaged the conquered countryside.[3] He may have negotiated the
peace terms in 1160; he certainly witnessed the document that
contained them. For the next two years he was often in France,
though miscellaneous documents issued or witnessed by him
from time to time show him at work in England.

During all these years he was carrying a burden of work of
which only a few traces can be seen in the records. Besides
being responsible for all receipts and outgoings at the exchequer,
and for the accounting twice yearly of the farms of the shires
and towns, he had charge of all ecclesiastical and feudal estates
that had lost their lord and not received his successor. He had,
also, much judicial business, either in the Curia Regis or when
on tour as an itinerant justice. Charters for towns passed through
his hands, as also the royal diplomatic correspondence. He
repaired the Tower of London between Easter and Whitsuntide
(? of 1156), flooding the works with carpenters and smiths.[4]
He received royal and other distinguished visitors on behalf of the
king. Beyond this, he had normally to be on hand with the king
wherever the court went with its chapel, and, as we have seen,
he acted as the king's military adviser and commander of his
army. In addition to this, he found time to accompany Henry
on some of his hunting and fowling expeditions, and to take
part in any sports and entertainments that were going forward.
The mere supervision and organization of his staff must have

1. W. FitzStephen, *MP.*, iii. 29–34.
2. Scutage had been levied in 1156 and earlier, but the amount now
raised was six times greater than before on church fees (J. H. Round,
Feudal England, 1895, 275–81). See also below, p. 47.
3. W. FitzStephen, *MB.*, iii. 34–5.
4. *MB.*, iii. 19–20.

taken much of his time. At maximum strength he had fifty-two clerks in action, and his writing-office, whose essential work could be done by two or three scribes, now had fifteen or more.[1]

We are better informed as to the personal and domestic detail of his life. Here the magnificence that he delighted in was remarked by all. For financial support he had the provostship of Beverley, prebends at Hastings, the revenue of the Tower of London, the castlery of Eye and the castle of Berkhampstead. He must also have made use, on his expenses account, of some of the vacant bishoprics, abbeys and fiefs.[2] With these great resources he entertained lavishly every day on gold and silver plate a multitude of guests. The food and drink was exquisite and very expensive, though we are told that he himself was sparing in its use. He was also generous in the extreme, giving away horses, garments and plate as well as minted money. When he crossed the Channel he had a convoy of six ships, and when the king took only one, Thomas gave him three more. England had long been noted for its wealth and abundance of precious things, and the age, indeed the whole of the later middle ages, delighted in a public display of wealth. This is true, and yet on more than one occasion at different times of his life, we seem to note in Thomas a love of the display of wealth and expensive things which is open to criticism, not only as unbecoming in a cleric and even in a devout Christian, but because there is in it a note of rhetoric, if not of vulgarity, that is inconsistent with a character of true dignity. Moreover, the instances of this in Thomas's life are not always explicable as the means chosen by an expert propagandist as the only, or at least the most effective way of gaining his end. Some of them, as we shall see, were criticized by contemporaries as errors of judgment, and a critic might say that ends that could be gained only in this way were, perhaps, not worthy of a wise man's efforts. One biographer, however,

1. *MB.*, iii. 29, and H. Bosham, *MB.*, iii. 176. T. A. M. Bishop, *Scriptores Regis*, Oxford, 1961, especially 9 ff., shows that fifteen separate scribes can be identified in Thomas's time as chancellor, whereas later in Henry's reign only two can be seen. For a discussion on writing-offices of the time, see *GF.*, 212.

2. John of Salisbury, writing in 1160, reminds Thomas that (according to rumour) he is receiving and using the revenues of three bishoprics uncanonically (*viz.* Exeter, Worcester and Coventry, *JS.*, *Ep.* 128, p. 223).

Herbert of Bosham, thought otherwise, and he may be allowed to speak:

'I will return to speak of his magnificence . . . for he was generous far beyond the demands of his high office, expansive to all, magnificent to all and beyond all, great of heart, great of stature and great in display. With him nothing would do but what was great in scale and magnificent in appearance.'[1]

Another, William FitzStephen, thus describes his embassy to Louis VII at Paris in 1158:

'In his company he had some two hundred horsemen, knights, clerks, stewards and men in waiting, men at arms and squires of noble family, all in ordered ranks. All these, and all their followers wore bright new festal garments. He also took twenty-four suits . . . and many silk cloaks to leave behind him as presents, and all kinds of parti-coloured clothes and foreign furs, hangings and carpets for a bishop's guest-room. Hounds and hawks were in the train . . . and eight five-horse chariots drawn by shire horses. On every horse was a sturdy groom in a new tunic, and on every chariot a warden. Two carts carried nothing but beer . . . for the French, who are not familiar with the brew, a healthy drink, clear, dark as wine, and finer in flavour. The chancellor's chapel had a special van, his private room another, his cash a third and his kitchen a fourth. Others bore food and drink, others dorsals, carpets, bags of night attire and luggage in general. He had twelve sumpter horses and eight chests of table plate, gold and silver. . . . One horse carried the plate, the altar furnishings, and the books of his chapel. . . . Every horse had a groom in smart turn-out; every chariot had a fierce great mastiff on a leash standing in the cart or walking beneath it, and every sumpter beast had a long-tailed monkey on its back. . . . Then there were about 250 men marching six or ten abreast, singing as they went in the English fashion. At intervals came braces of staghounds and greyhounds with their attendants, . . . then the men at arms, with the shields and chargers of the knights, then other men at arms and boys and men carrying hawks.'

All these were far from being the total numbers of the procession, and

'Last of all came the chancellor and some of his friends. . . . Arrived in Paris . . . he loaded every baron, knight, . . . master, scholar and burgess with gifts of plate, clothing, horses and money.'[2]

1. H. Bosham, *MB.*, iii. 176.
2. W. FitzStephen, *MB.*, iii. 29–33.

How much of this, we wonder, was paid for by the abbeys and bishoprics that were 'in the king's hand'?

During all these years his intimate friendship with the king endured. They rode together, hunted and hawked together, and together perhaps indulged in the pleasures—which throughout the middle ages had a slightly raffish air—of a game of chess.[1] FitzStephen tells how the king sometimes came to the chancellor's hall to see its latest splendours. Sometimes he rode in on horseback, sometimes fresh from the hunt with arrows in his hand. On one day he would take a drink and be gone at once; on another he would leap the table and sit for a meal next to his host.[2] Once again we think of another Henry supping with another Thomas at Chelsea, and walking in his garden with his arm about More's neck. A final sign of his high esteem was to entrust to his chancellor his eldest son Henry, to join the company of boys and youths of baronial family who were being brought up under his supervision. All, not only his biographers, but such as John of Salisbury and Gilbert Foliot in their letters, speak of him as holding all power in the kingdom, as Joseph with Pharaoh.

In these years of achievement and success the chancellor often found himself trying to serve two masters. In public he was the king's all-powerful minister and confidant, closer to his master, so it seemed, in sympathy and aim, than even Abbot Suger had been to the king of France or Rainald of Dassel was to be to Barbarossa. Yet he kept at least a sector of his life to himself. He remained entirely chaste in his private life, despite the example of the king.[3] He preserved ecclesiastics and monks when he could from some of the king's exactions, and was a principal benefactor of Merton when the canons built the eastern limb of their church. His biographer notes that he was sparing in his personal diet, that he prayed often at night in his bedchamber and visited churches in the early dawn.[4] He also commissioned

---

1. W. FitzStephen, *MB.*, iii. 25. The scene in Tennyson's *Becket* is familiar.
2. *MB.*, iii. 25.
3. W. FitzStephen, *MB.*, iii. 21; Anonymous I, *MB.*, iv. 13–4; William of Canterbury i. 6. The last is followed by Guernes, who alone gives the name, Avice of Stafford, of the woman concerned, and the place, Stoke-on-Trent (*GW.*, lines 301 ff.).
4. The twilight visit to a church is in *Thómas Saga*, RS., i. 51, 53.

two secular priests, who are named, one at Canterbury, the other in London, to scourge him penitentially; this was a practice which he kept up as archbishop and intensified during his exile.[1]

These years as chancellor deserve careful consideration as the background of what followed. During them Thomas had, within the context of that age, all but supreme power in administration and patronage, as well as financial control and important judicial office. After initial difficulties, he had had great success in dealing with great men and great affairs. He had met and treated with barons of every social type as equals and colleagues in the king's service. He had come to know the bishops and the heads of the greater religious houses, and had on occasion treated them *de haut en bas*. To all these men he had appeared principally as a king's man and a brilliant executant of large plans. He was known also as one apt to put royal policy before church law or custom. As has already been noted, he held a position of trust and power such as had never before been held by a subject in England, and was not to be held again until the days of Wolsey. Like Wolsey, he had held it with loyalty and brilliance, and, unlike Wolsey, he had given no offence by overbearing assurance or by purely personal acquisition of riches.

(ii) The Chancellor and the Church

In 1157 Thomas as Chancellor took part in an episode which to some contemporaries and many historians has seemed to show a conduct inconsistent with his principles and practice as archbishop. This was the plea for exemption from episcopal surveillance on the part of the abbey of Battle, and the events cannot be understood without a glance at the past history of 'exemption' within the monastic body.

From the birth of organized monachism in the fourth century till the tenth century and beyond, the monastery, like all other ecclesiastical persons and institutes, normally lay within the jurisdiction of the bishop of the diocese or region. Nevertheless, by its very nature it had remained outside the currents of diocesan life, and it had been recognised that when all went well, it would

1. For the scourgings, see evidence of Robert of Merton in E. Grim, *MB.*, ii. 418, and W. FitzStephen, *MB.*, iii. 22.

be left to follow its rule without interference. Such was the position as made clear in the Rule of St Benedict,[1] and so long as the monastery was relatively small, and contained few, if any clerics, no difficulty arose. But when monks proceeded in large numbers to Holy Orders, and the monastery became a large and complex establishment, controlling wide estates, it became, in the feudal, fragmented Europe from the eighth century onward, a desirable object for spoil and absorption both to the territorial lord and to the regional bishop. The king or lord in the epoch of the proprietary church sought to exploit or even suppress the house; the bishop sought to absorb the abbey either by himself acting as (absentee) abbot while using the revenues, or by occupying the whole establishment as his cathedral or abusing its hospitality for ordinations, synods and other assemblies. The monastery, for its part, had two remedies: it might be commended to the king or local lord and receive various degrees of immunity from outside interference, or it might petition the pope for a bull restraining the bishop from touching the place. The former, in the decentralisation of all authority in the dark ages, was at first more frequent and effective; the latter was often of little practical value, but the Roman documents and the papacy itself survived all shocks, and the future lay with this policy, though often only after centuries in which it had been inoperative. In each class there was a sub-species of distinction. Certain monasteries all over Europe became royal or imperial monasteries *par excellence*, while from the foundation of Cluny onwards the practice of commendation and the payment of census to the papacy gave to Rome a peculiar interest in the protection of the abbey concerned. Cluny is an eminent example. When, in the twelfth century, the centralizing papacy was reviving and redefining canonical sanctions, the concept of 'exemption' replaced that of belonging to (the Church of) St Peter, and was expressed in various formulas, of which the phrase *nullo mediante* (i.e. subject to the Holy See *directly*) was signalized by Alexander III (1159–81) as decisive.

In England at the time of the Conquest several abbeys had royal immunity and several treasured papal privileges of questionable authenticity. Among them Westminster and certain other royal churches had as 'royal chapels' (later called 'royal peculiars')

1. *Benedicti Regula*, chaps. lxii, lxiv.

a *de facto* exemption from every other authority in Church and State. When the Conqueror founded Battle on the site of his victory of 1066 he gave it, probably implicitly or by word of mouth, the status of a royal chapel or *Eigenkirche*, though it is unlikely that a formal charter was issued stating this.[1] In the half-century that followed, this status was preserved without serious controversy or precise definition, though at some time the monks wrote up and embellished charters of the Conqueror and his successors. During this period, also, both bishops of Chichester and abbots of Battle acted in the interests of peace in ways inconsistent with the positions they adopted in controversy.

At last a serious clash occurred when Hilary of Chichester (bishop 1147–69), who had lived and practised for some years at the Curia and was familiar with recent canonical developments, attempted to assert his right of visitation and the abbot's obligation to attend his synods. To enforce his claims he sought from Eugenius III and Hadrian IV bulls instructing the abbot, under pain of excommunication, to acknowledge episcopal jurisdiction, and as the abbey had no papal privileges the bishop's wish was granted. After some time, however, the abbot of the day, Walter de Luci, brother of Richard de Luci, justiciar, appealed to Henry II, relying on the fabricated royal charters to establish his status as a royal chapel. After various delays the case was heard by a strong gathering of the inner royal council at Colchester abbey in 1157. The long account of this in the 'Battle Chronicle' can be matched only by that of the trial of William of St Carilef eighty years earlier, and is probably in its main lines authentic. Thomas, as chancellor, had a considerable part to play. Bishop Hilary was driven back from his arguments as to past practice and tried to hold his line on the papal letters instructing him to enforce submission to episcopal authority, but he was injudicious enough to treat the king and his council to an exposition of the Gelasian doctrine of papal

1. The case is recounted at length in *Chronicon Monasterii de Bello*, ed. J. S. Brewer, London 1846, 84–104 (Anglia Christiana Society). It has often been discussed, most recently by H. Mayr-Harting, 'Hilary. Bishop of Chichester, and Henry II', in *EHR.*, lxxviii. (April, 1963), 209–24. The charters have been critically examined by Eleanor Searle, in 'Battle Abbey and exemption: the forged charters', in *EHR.* lxxxiii, (July, 1968), 449–80.

power, which was angrily interrupted by the king. When Hilary denied the royal right to depose abbots, Henry exclaimed: 'Depose, No; shove out, Yes', and proceeded to give a pantomime of the process. Henry was supported by his chancellor, who summed up the royal case, accepting the abbey's charters as genuine, and pressed it home against the bishop, who finally submitted. Eleven years later, when relations between Thomas and Henry had reached a deadlock of hostility, the archbishop mentioned this case to the pope as an instance of the king's oppressive demands that the Church should submit to royal control,[1] and historians in general have remarked that the Battle incident is an example of the facility with which Becket could change his principles to suit his official position. We may agree that Thomas the chancellor and Thomas the archbishop viewed —or at least expounded—a single incident in different ways, and to that extent showed inconsistency, but it is not necessary to regard the difference of approach as hypocritical, or either attitude as indefensible. Much water had flowed under the bridges between 1157 and 1168, both of the Thames and of the Tiber. In 1157 the canonical attitude to exemption had not become settled; still less had any general *modus vivendi* been established. The curial practice under Eugenius and Hadrian was normally to stress the canonical rights of the bishop, save in the clear cases of papal privilege. The Roman officials were perfectly correct in denying a privileged position to Battle, though Hilary had probably procured his letters by means of a considerable economy of truth. On the other hand, the conception of a royal *Eigenkirche* was familiar to French, German and English kings, and no papal move had been made against the institution as such. It is still to-day the basic explanation of the anomalous ecclesiastical status of Westminster Abbey and St Margaret's. Even if the muniments of Battle had been forged, the rights had certainly been globally bestowed by the Conqueror and had been used sporadically ever since. This was not one of the planks of the reform party or of Thomas at any time of his life. And in the event Battle, along with Westminster and other houses, slipped over the fence into the list of canonically exempt houses. It was Hilary, clever and tactless as ever, who was prepared to abandon his position when it proved unacceptable to the king.

1. *MB.*, vii. (643), 242.

Archbishop Theobald had been a principal influence with the young king in his appointment of Thomas as chancellor, and his principal motive had been to secure the freedom and just demands of the Church as against secular and royal encroachment. How far were his hopes realised? We have no inkling of what passed in Thomas's mind during those years. We do not know whether he was led into what seem to be the paths of ambition and personal satisfaction by the allurements of power and wealth, or whether he sincerely thought that he could hold to essentials best by going part of the way with Henry. Several actions or decisions of policy seem to contradict this last supposition.

There is, first, his administration under the king of vacant bishoprics and abbacies. This *regale*, familiar in feudal countries for the greater part of the middle ages and beyond, was not customary in England before the Conquest, and it had never been formally countenanced by the Church. FitzStephen denied that Thomas was to blame in delaying elections and engrossing the revenues for the royal administration, but in another place Herbert of Bosham belies this defence of Thomas in his statement that at Theobald's death the chancellor was given the administration of the see, as he had been given on all similar occasions, and the vacancy endured for a year.[1] We have also the explicit statement of FitzStephen that the chancellor maintained a large number of clerks, perhaps fifteen or twenty, in the administration of such benefices.

Next, there is the matter of scutage, that is, the tax on a knight's fee which was gradually substituted for a demand for personal feudal service. A scutage was levied in 1156 for the king's war against his brother Geoffrey. It was not the first time a scutage had been taken, and on this occasion, as previously, it was levied principally on the feudal estates of the Church, and it appears that Theobald protested, though in vain. How far the chancellor was responsible for this particular levy is not known. A heavier and more universal scutage was taken for the war of Toulouse in 1159, and now the tax was heavier on ecclesiastics than on others. Hence the point of Gilbert Foliot's bitter invective, seven years

1. For Bosham's admissions, see *MB.*, iii. 180 and 299. For FitzStephen's denial, see *MB.*, iii. 23, which is implicitly contradicted by his admissions *ibid.*, 29 and 54–5. See also John of Salisbury *MB.*, v. (9), 14 and cf. p. 39 n. 2 above.

later, when he accused Thomas of plunging a sharp sword into
the vitals of his mother the Church, and maintained that a chief
reason for the general acquiescence in his election was that he
would then be unable to repeat the performance. The dates are
not in Foliot's favour, for three full years had passed between
the Toulouse scutage and the election, but the immediate indignation was certainly widespread and John of Salisbury, while
defending the archbishop (also in 1166) and denying that the
tax was due to his initiative, admitted his responsibility for
accepting and exploiting it.[1] Historians to-day, who are themselves
unwilling taxpayers on a scale familiar in the middle ages only
to those in the hands of usurers, are usually censorious both of
medieval grumblers and of ecclesiastical privilege, and tend to
be favourable to the chancellor, but on his own principles Thomas
would seem here to stand condemned.

A third accusation is the chancellor's reluctance to accept
Theobald's prohibition of a 'second aid' tax levied by the archdeacon on the churches of his diocese.[2] Here again there would
seem to be little to be said in Thomas's defence, for the tax
merely swelled the revenues of the chancellor[3].

Finally, there is the failure of Thomas to surrender the archdeaconry of Canterbury when chancellor, and his failure to
respond to Theobald's death-bed summons to visit him, which
he eluded by what seems to have been collusive action between
Thomas and John of Salisbury in alleging important royal
business in excuse. These two last charges, perhaps, weigh
against him more than any others in the minds of modern readers
of his story.[4]

Some years after Thomas's arrival at Canterbury, the group of
clerks round the archbishop was joined by a newcomer, recommended to Theobald by no less a personage than St Bernard,
and one whose gifts and reputation give him a place apart in any

1. John of Salisbury, writing to Bartholomew of Exeter in 1166, curses
the tax, but absolves Thomas (*MB.*, v. (194), 378–9). Foliot, in his
letter *Multiplicem* (*MB.*, v. (225), 525), accuses Thomas of plunging a
sword into the vitals of the Church. See A. Saltman, *Theobald, Archbishop
of Canterbury*, London 1956, 44–5, and John of Salisbury's letter to
Thomas in *JS.*, *Ep.*, 128.
2. For this see *JS.*, *Ep.*, 22 and C. N. L. Brooke's notes.
3. *TL.*, 161–3.
4. *JS.*, *Epp.*, 128, 129, with C. N. L. Brooke's comments, p. xxxvii.

picture of the age. John of Salisbury was an almost exact contemporary of Thomas. In 1147 he was a young man of thirty. By that time he had recently completed his long years of study in philosophy and theology at Chartres and Paris and elsewhere (1135–45/7). This was followed by a short stay as secretary or counsellor to his friend Peter, Abbot of Celle, and it was then that he received from St Bernard a letter of recommendation to Theobald. According to the most probable of several reconstructions of his movements[1], he was received by Theobald in some capacity in 1147, and remained in England for a year or so, accompanying the archbishop at the council of Rheims and the subsequent trial of his old master, Gilbert de la Porrée. He then went to the papal court in Italy, and remained there till 1153, returning in the autumn to become Theobald's most trusted counsellor and secretary, except for a short interval, till the archbishop's death in 1161. On this reckoning he would have been a colleague of Thomas at Canterbury some years before the accession of Henry II, though his duties at Theobald's side may have given little occasion for close companionship. In any case, when evidence becomes available, the two are friends, and they remained so until the end.

Though friends, they were men of very different gifts and characters, and there is no evidence that their friendship was intimate. John of Salisbury, the most elaborately furnished mind of the age and an eminent example of the humane, unprofessional education that he advocated so persuasively, remained well on this side of idolatry in the presence of even the greatest of his contemporaries, such as Abelard, Gilbert de la Porrée, Bernard and Thomas himself. If not precisely a peacemaker, he was certainly no trouble-raiser, and in all matters he worked for calm and deliberation. As we shall see, he stood firmly on Thomas's side in essentials, and had, indeed, suffered in the cause of the Church while the chancellor was still unregenerate, but there were elements of impetuosity and immoderation in his friend's character which he did not share, while Thomas for his part lacked the learning and the literary tact of John. During the chancellorship John accepted his friend's authority and magnificence, though when Theobald was dying his secretary's loyalty

1. *JS.*, pp. xv–xix; A. Saltman, *Theobald, Archbishop of Canterbury,* London 1956, 169 ff.

ut a strain upon his relations with the powerful minister who
eemed forgetful of his old patron.

Theobald had been an invalid for some time before his death.
When he realized that the end was near he wrote urgently and
repeatedly to Thomas to come to him while there was yet time.
The chancellor was engaged abroad; he may or may not have
influenced the king to stress his need for his minister's services.
In any case, he did not return to receive Theobald's farewell,
and if there is not sufficient evidence to convict him of insensi-
tivity and ingratitude, there is certainly none to show the piety to
which John appealed.[1]

1. Letters of Theobald, *JS.*, *Epp.*, 128, 129 and notes.

CHAPTER 5

The Archbishop

(i) The Archbishop at Canterbury

A YEAR elapsed before Canterbury again had a pontiff, and during this time the chancellor administered, in the king's interest and his own, the revenues of the see which he was so well acquainted.[1] The length of this interval must be remembered in any discussion of the election that ended it; the long delay rules out any suggestion of a stampede. The simplest explanation is that Henry, who was absent from England for most of the time and who was occupied with many things, was content to receive the ample Canterbury revenues for as long as possible, and that the chancellor was restrained from interference both for a similar motive and also because he must have known from the first of the possibility of his own appointment. Long before, Theobald had thought of him as a possible successor,[2] and we have the definite assertion of two biographers that general rumour had selected him.[3] The field, to the many who surveyed it, must have seemed remarkably empty. There was a tradition that the archbishop should be a monk. It was a shaky tradition, but the outstanding instances of Augustine, Dunstan, Alphege, Lanfranc and Anselm had given it power, and it was supported by the community of Christ Church, the electoral body. Translation of a bishop was rarer than in later centuries, but not unknown, and the two most eminent of the bishops were Cluniac monks, Henry of Winchester and Gilbert of Hereford. Henry, however, after years of action and intrigue, was now an elder statesman, and the young king would wish for an archbishop with whom he could work well.

1. H. Bosham, *MB.*, iii. 180.
2. William of Canterbury, *MB.*, i. 4.
3. Emphatically H. Bosham, *MB.*, iii. 180; more vaguely William of Canterbury, *MB.*, i. 8.

None of the sources mentions any third party besides Gilbert and Thomas as a likely choice.

One of Thomas's well-informed biographers tells us that a visitor to the chancellor at Rouen, the prior of Leicester, spoke to him of the rumours of his election; this was probably in January 1162.[1] But Thomas had no direct knowledge of the king's intention till he was about to go to England on the king's business in May, primarily and ostensibly to obtain the homage of the barons to the 'young king' Henry. All the biographers agree that he at once expressed his reluctance, as foreseeing the rupture that would take place between himself and the king, and there is no reason to suspect his sincerity. He was in a position of outstanding importance, and knew well that he had made a success of his opportunities. One side of his nature and character had fulfilled itself, and if, as seems certain, his deeper self was uneasy in a life of merely worldly activity and display, an uneasy conscience would scarcely suggest an escape by way of an archbishopric.

Henry, however, with a lack of insight equal, though diametrically opposite, to that of Theobald in 1154, held to his course, convinced that he could control an archbishop as he had controlled or charmed a chancellor. Herbert of Bosham, who records what he had often heard from Thomas himself, tells us that the latter had long guessed what Henry had intended to do, and had remonstrated with him.[2] Henry replied by announcing his decision openly to Richard de Luci and the other commissioners who were returning with the chancellor to England. They were commanded to carry forward the election as firmly as they would swear loyalty to the young prince. Thomas yielded at last, owing in part to the pressure of the cardinal legate, Henry of Pisa, a Cistercian.[3] Arrived in England, the commissioners Richard de Luci, one of the two justiciars, Walter, abbot of Battle, his brother, and bishops Bartholomew of Exeter, Hilary of Chichester and Walter of Rochester, went to Canterbury to win the chapter of monks, most of whom must have known Thomas well. Considerable resistance was shown to one who was neither a monk nor, seemingly, a man of learning or spirituality, but ultimately the vote was given in his favour. The matter

1. W. FitzStephen, *MB.*, iii. 25–6.
2. H. Bosham, *MB.*, iii. 180–1.
3. John of Salisbury, *MB.*, ii. 306.

was then taken back to Westminster, where the bishops and
abbots of the province were asked for their assent. Here again
there were difficulties, but agreement was ultimately reached
with all save Gilbert Foliot supporting Thomas. The elect was
then freed of all his obligations incurred as chancellor, was
ordained priest on 2 June, and consecrated by Henry of Winchester on the following day, the first Sunday after Pentecost
which the monks kept as their patronal festival of the Blessed
Trinity. Fourteen bishops of the province were present, re-
presenting all the sees save the vacant see of London. Thomas
was forty-four years and five months old. Subsequently a small
party consisting of John of Salisbury, Adam, abbot of Evesham
and another, travelled out to Montpellier for the *pallium*.

When, four years later, the great quarrel was at its most bitter
climax, Gilbert Foliot, then bishop of London and the acknowledged leader of the party opposed to the archbishop, accused
him of bribing himself into the chancellorship as a springboard
to the archbishopric, of hastening back to England on Theobald's
death to prepare the ground for his own election, and of persuading
the king to press him as candidate. The election duly took place
according to Foliot, solely through the royal threats, and from
fear of worse to come from those who opposed the royal will.
Yet, despite the royal pressure, the declarations of opinion hostile
to Thomas were many and strong, but ultimately almost all
yielded to *force majeure*.[1] To this Thomas returned a flat denial.
All the stages of his election had been lawfully performed. No
public protest of any kind had occurred. If some had opposed the
election it had been *in camera*, and their motive may well have
been disappointed ambition. In any case, the election had been
declared unanimous, and everyone concerned in it had joined
in applying to the pope for the *pallium*.[2]

Despite the apparent contradictions, these two accounts can be
largely harmonized. The acquisition of the chancellorship has
already been discussed. The office had never been regarded as a
step towards the archbishopric. Nor had Thomas's conduct in
office suggested that this was his aim. Neither his treatment
of the Church, nor his unclerical behaviour, nor his material

1. So Gilbert Foliot, *MB.*, v. (205) 408 ff.; *GFL*, no. 167; developed
later in *Multiplicem*.
2. So Thomas, *MB.*, v. (223), 490 ff., especially 498.

exploits could have been a recommendation to his electors or
a sign of his desire for high spiritual office. Modern historians
carry in their memories the exactly contemporary career of
Rainald of Dassel (born 1118), who became chancellor to Frederick
Barbarossa in 1156 and archbishop of Cologne in 1159, and even
if no contemporary writer drew the parallel, it is possible that
Henry, whose mother knew Germany well, may have been
encouraged by the example. Thomas's return to England was not,
in fact, precipitate; it was made at the king's command, when
almost a year had elapsed since the demise of Theobald. That
he had supreme power and could, therefore, persuade the king
and veto any candidate except himself was a gratuitous charge
against his integrity on the part of Foliot.[1] But, when all this has
been said, it must be allowed that the biographers provide
evidence that the election did not proceed smoothly. Externally
and officially events may have taken place, as Thomas said,
without a hitch. We may even allow that the canonical secrecy
surrounding an episcopal election was partly observed while the
archbishop was still alive, but that there was opposition besides
that of Foliot himself, is certain.

The entry into office at Canterbury of Thomas of London
was marked by a transformation of his way of life which the
biographers describe as putting off the old man, and transformation into another man. Accepting these phrases without more ado,
most of those who have written of Thomas in the past eighty
years have accepted a total change of the whole man, which they
then endeavour to explain. The explanation most in favour is that
which was first propounded, it would seem, by Radford, the
careful historian of Thomas of London. In order to defend
Thomas from an alleged lack of consistency, which he somewhat
surprisingly assumed to 'be the one quality which the world
requires most rigidly of its great statesmen', he undertook to
show that the apparent inconsistencies of Thomas were, in fact,
parts of a consistent endeavour to suit his actions to the demands
of his office for the time being.[2] This conception was given a
slightly different turn by Mrs (later Lady) Stenton in her early
(1926) and very influential chapter in the *Cambridge Medieval*

---

1. *MB.*, v. (225), 524–5.
2. *TL.*, 233. Writing in 1892–3, was he thinking of Mr Gladstone? Or
of Joseph Chamberlain?

History.[1] To her Thomas Becket was a skilful actor who could play to perfection any part; to-day the extroverted, jovial, efficient administrator, to-morrow the ascetic archbishop. This conception, considerably deepened, was put forward by another influential historian, Professor Z. N. Brooke,[2] who avoided any suggestion of hypocrisy or conscious play-acting, but saw in Becket one who grasped clearly what would now be called the 'image' of a chancellor and an archbishop, and skilfully, one might even say admirably, reproduced those images in himself.

It may be thought that all these and similar interpretations are artificial and in varying degrees superficial. Thomas's conduct has a simpler, more human, and yet a more spiritual explanation. In the first place, the change in May 1162, was not, by the evidence of the very group of biographers who propagated the phrase, a transformation or a rebirth of character. Thomas had never been a libertine, an unbeliever, a rogue or a trickster. His biographers agree that he had always lived chastely, even in face of strong allurement, and although he was bound by no public vow. The conversion of life, if such there was, took place when he left his post in the city of London for Theobald's household. That was tantamount to choosing the career of an observant clerk, with the prospect of the priesthood, if not of the episcopate, and under the rule of the austere and monastic Theobald real, not affected, piety was expected. The only fault which the biographers hint at is ambition. In his chancellorship we hear of incidents which show a deep religious purpose. He rose to prayer at night, when others were asleep, and in the early dawn at the church-door; he caused himself to be frequently scourged and was lavish in almsgiving. He is certainly charged with visible external faults as chancellor; of ruthlessness against those who threatened the king's power, of ostentatious extravagance, of extortion, of ingratitude and unfeeling conduct towards his old master; of neglecting the spiritual office of archdeacon in order to extend his activities as chancellor above all, of vanity and worldly behaviour. These accusations are difficult to evaluate; most of them could be made of any great minister, but they are probably valid.

1. Vol. v. (1926), chap. xvii.
2. Z. N. Brooke, *The English Church and the Papacy*, Cambridge 1931, 193–4.

The picture that emerges is of a boy schooled in childhood by a devout mother; of a schoolboy following the round of a religious house; of a young man who kept himself within the bounds of sincere moral and religious practice. He had great abilities, of which he must gradually have become aware. He had also a personality of great natural charm and great flexibility, which could take the colour of his surroundings and imitate the manners and interests of those whom he admired or served without revealing his own deepest aspirations. Among the group of brilliant and acquisitive young and middle-aged men in Theobald's household he himself became ambitious and acquisitive; later, as chancellor, now the equal of great ones in Church and State, and the personal friend and companion of an unusually gifted young king, he deployed all his exceptional talents to please and satisfy his master. He was willing to go very far in helping the king to gain control over the Church. But in all this he remained fundamentally dissatisfied with himself. When the archbishopric became a possibility, he was divided in mind. He was sincerely apprehensive of his weakness and of the contest with the king that was bound to come. On the other hand, besides the inevitable challenge of such high office, and the knowledge that he alone knew what was in the king's mind, there was the attraction of a post in which for the first time in his life he could put spiritual claims firmly before worldly interests. When the fateful consent had been given, it was not a case of imitating a model or an imagined code of action for an archbishop, but of being for the first time free to follow the call which he had long heard and neglected. It was now his task to live the life of a priest and bishop as familiar to him from the Scriptures, the liturgy, and Christian tradition, and as seen in the context of twelfth-century religious sentiment, in which the monastic ideal was paramount. Thomas's life is, indeed, a striking example of the acceptance of a vocation by one who has long delayed in giving all to the service of Christ, and who has seemed to onlookers to be giving all to the world till the moment of resolve came. It is a shape of life far from uncommon; Thomas rendered it uncommon by the force and perseverance with which he drove himself along the new path, with the sense of his long refusal always before him.

His habit of life at Canterbury is described at length by Herbert of Bosham, whom he had chosen as his confidant and mentor as they rode away from his acceptance of office.[1] Herbert has come in for some hard words from editors and historians as 'one of the most provoking of authors', the composer of 'tedious superfluities' and of 'long, dull and, unmeaning' narratives, which he begs future editors to leave intact, though he may, as a near contemporary remarks, 'weave an immense web of verbiage'.[2] Recent scholarship has redressed the balance somewhat by showing that his scriptural learning was great, and there must have been more than a little worth in the mind and character of one whom archbishop Thomas could keep so near to himself for so long. In any case, we can scarcely disbelieve his factual statements as to the archbishop's daily life.

Thomas rose to the Office in the small hours, and afterwards in secret washed the feet of thirteen poor men. He slept again for a short time, and then studied Scripture with Herbert's assistance; then Herbert retired and the archbishop prayed alone. He did not celebrate Mass daily, refraining from reverence, but when he celebrated, it was with great devotion, preparing himself with the prayers of St Anselm, and celebrating rapidly. Next, he heard any cases that might be pending in the archbishop's court, and only after this, about midday, went to his hall for dinner. There his household clerks sat on his right, and a group of monks and religious on his left. At his side his crossbearer read Scripture or some Latin work. In front, at some distance to save them from the tedium of hearing a language which they did not understand, his knights dined at a table by themselves, with special dishes to compensate them for missing the reading. Serving the archbishop and his guests were the boys of baronial family who learnt manners and the accomplishments of their class in the archbishop's retinue. Among them the young prince Henry served Thomas himself. The whole dining-hall was magnificent, wrote Herbert, magnificent in the company, in the waiters, and in the servers, and most magnificent of all in the festal meats. Thomas himself fared simply, without careful choice of food, and drinking a little wine. No one could see or suspect the monastic habit and the hairshirt under the canon's simple rochet that he wore. After dining he retired with his

1. H. Bosham, *MB.*, iii. 186.
2. J. C. Robertson, introduction to his Life in *MB.*, iii. pp. xxiii–xxv.

learned clerks to a discussion of Scripture or some practical
moral problem.[1]

Like his predecessor, he had the services of a brilliant staff,
of whom Herbert provides a list.[2] At the head was Lombard of
Piacenza, a trained canonist, teacher of Herbert and the archbishop alike. Named cardinal in 1171, he was appointed archbishop of Benevento. John of Salisbury, the most brilliant of all,
had been secretary and *alter ego* to archbishop Theobald, and
was a member of Thomas's *familia* till 1163, when he was exiled.
Robert Foliot, a member of the Foliot clan and sometime archdeacon of Oxford (1151–74), was at Canterbury for the early
years of Thomas's episcopate, but did not follow him into exile.
He became bishop of Hereford in 1174, and died in 1186.
Reginald FitzJocelin, son of Jocelin de Bohun, bishop of
Salisbury, and known as the Lombard, probably from the region
of his birth, must have been a junior member of the household
(he was born in 1140–1). He followed Thomas abroad, but defected
to his father in 1166 and was later one of the royal 'promotion'
of 1173, receiving the see of Bath. Elected archbishop of Canterbury
in November 1191, he died a month later. Gerard la Pucelle,
another young member, was clerked and presented to his first
benefice by archbishop Thomas, but left the household, though
remaining in close touch with John of Salisbury. He was later
bishop of Coventry for a year, 1183–4. Hugh de Nonant, nephew
of Arnulf of Lisieux, and himself archdeacon of that city, was
yet another young clerk at Canterbury. He defected only in 1170
and in time followed Gerard at Coventry, 1188–98. A fourth
young man, Gilbert de Glanville, remained faithful and ultimately
became bishop of Rochester, 1185–1214. There were others: Ralph
of Sarre, dean of Rheims from 1170; Jordan of Melbourne, dean
of Chichester; Mathew of Chichester, archdeacon and later also
dean of that cathedral; Philip of Calne, a Londoner, who studied
theology and canon law at Tours; Humbert the Lombard from
Milan, who became in turn archdeacon of Bourges, archbishop of
Milan and finally Pope Urban III. Finally there was Alexander
Llewellyn the archbishop's cross-bearer and personal sacristan,
witty and outspoken, who gave his master firm advice at

1. All this is in Herbert's *Life*, *MB.*, iii. 189–247.
2. *MB.*, iii. 523–530.

Northampton. There can have been few bishops in Europe with a more distinguished household.

(ii) Church and King

When Thomas of London accepted his election to Canterbury as the king's nominee he was firmly convinced, and with reason, that he would soon be involved in controversy with his late master. The reasons for the tragic quarrel that ensued were certainly due in part to the temperaments and limitations of the two chief actors, but the essential cause was deeper, reflecting in both king and prelate a difference of outlook that had divided Europe for a century and more.

We have seen on an earlier page how deeply entwined in English life before the Conquest were the functions and offices of Church and royal power. In this they reflected, though with considerable national peculiarities, the old state of things throughout Europe. In western Europe for many centuries after the conversion of Constantine, the Church, and in particular the city-bishops, had the legal right of ownership of lands and revenues such as was possessed by any other person or body. The Church was also autonomous in the sense that its bishops were freely elected in the manner customary to each region, and the right of confirmation claimed by emperors with regard to the papacy and a few other important sees was never formally acknowledged and disappeared with the escape of the west from the eastern sphere of government. For a few centuries, indeed, in Italy and Gaul, the bishops, and above all the papacy, were in effect either independent rulers or governors of their cities under the Merovingian kings.

The situation changed in the eighth century when the Carolingian empire was being established and feudalism gradually spread and developed. On the political level this resulted in the theory and practice that the territories of the empire were bestowed upon landowners, both lay and clerical, by the monarch in return for certain services, and on the demise of the vassal reverted to the giver. As the gift of lands normally carried all kinds of rights of revenue and jurisdiction, the great feudal tenants and vassals, clerical as well as lay, were closely tied to the lay power by feudal homage, and by the exercise of administrative powers as

as well as by their obligation to give counsel and help. The
monarch for his part, especially Charlemagne and his immediate
successors, regarded himself as holding under God the right
and duty of governing the Christian people, a right which carried
with it the duty and power of appointing bishops. The papacy,
holding as it did an independent political position far away in
Italy, was regarded as the ultimate authority in doctrine and
discipline, which in the epoch of papal decadence could in
practice be ignored. This involvement of the Church in secular
government was made more complete by the gradual spread of
private, that is, normally lay, ownership over the whole Church.
This lay control varied in character from region to region. In
England, as we have seen, the interpenetration of what must be
called, for want of a better phrase, Church and State was thorough-
going, but at the same time the monarch's part in the control of
church matters was loose and easy. In the German kingdom,
on the other hand, where the great bishoprics were powerful
dukedoms, the control was very tight, and the monarch appointed
bishops, receiving from the elect feudal homage, and investing
him in return with the church, i.e. the lands of the church, with
all their rights and obligations. The fact that a large sum of
money often passed between the elect and the monarch gave the
transaction the stigma of simony in the eyes of later reformers,
but even without this the investiture was clear evidence of lay
control. Even the papacy was on occasion treated thus as a part
of the property of the empire.

When, in the eleventh century, the religious revival and conse-
quent spiritual and moral awakening affected institutions and
politics and became the 'Gregorian reform', the lay control of
the Church and in particular the customary rights of the Empire
and other kingdoms were in the fore-front of the controversy.
Gradually with the reform of the papacy and the disentanglement
of the Church from lay control, and the development of the clergy
as a class with laws and privileges and a strong centralised
authority facing the civil governments of Europe, a tension was
everywhere set up and the great ideological controversy of western
Europe, the struggle between the papacy and the Empire, developed. In the ferment of new life both ecclesiastical and secular
institutions developed rapidly. At the same time the spiritual
rebirth, made evident by the increase of the monastic order and

of secular canons, as well as by the universal building or rebuilding of churches, made the twelfth century an age of faith *par excellence*, an age in which both Catholic faith and discipline had a greater influence upon the minds and actions of men than at any other time in the middle ages, imposing sanctions and ideals upon all, whatever their practice might be. The tensions of the great struggle were increased by the circumstance that the new ecclesiastical ideology, while claiming with much justice to be merely the ancient, traditional way, was, in fact, erupting in a world saturated with the thoughts and habits of centuries of contrary practice. Moreover, it was not a case of one political theory fighting another. While kings and administrators were going their way along roads worn by centuries of custom, the papacy and its followers were declaring a rigid set of disciplinary laws without, at first, any consideration of what was practicable and acceptable or equitable. Moreover, the minds at the centre of the reform, largely Italian or French, had from the first an element of intransigence, of unbending logicality that often tended to push principles beyond the capabilities of normal life. Thus, the contest often became one of new discipline versus old custom, and among the rulers of the Germanic and Scandinavian half of Europe law that was not custom was almost inconceivable.

Nowhere was the division of outlook more sharp than in England. As has been seen, there had been under the Old English kings an inextricable mingling of Church and State under a monarchy which was comparatively strong in the machinery of administration, but easy in its relations with the Church. England was still almost untouched by the Italian reform and English churchmen had little or no familiarity with Rome save as a place of pilgrimage, though some English bishops had recently attended synods of the reforming popes. Similarly, Duke William before 1066 had done much to regularise and reform the Church in his duchy, but kept his bishops and abbots, whose appointments he controlled, firmly in hand. Once settled in England, his intention was to reform the Church, now integrated into the feudal network, but to preserve all the royal powers within the ring-fence of his island kingdom and Norman dukedom. This implied a resistance to what he regarded as encroachment by the papacy. Under Lanfranc, who shared his views, his policy was eminently successful. The Conqueror, indeed, acted much in the fashion of Charlemagne or one of the devout German kings such as Henry II, and Gregory VII had the wisdom to allow his version of reform to continue without disturbance.

Under William II there were changes both in England and at Rome. Although recent scholarship has reduced some of the charges of oppression and unprecedented extortion made against Rufus by monastic writers, there is no doubt that he exploited the feudal status of bishops and abbots by using his control of elections and right of protection during vacancies to keep sees and abbeys vacant while appropriating the revenues. Meanwhile, under Popes Urban II (1088–99) and more particularly Paschal II (1099–1118), the leading Gregorian ideas had been developed and expressed and the number of reforming bishops had multiplied. Consequently Anselm, appointed by William II when seriously ill, differed greatly from Lanfranc in his attitude to papal instructions. In exile for opposition to William II, he absorbed the whole papal programme including the matter of investiture. When Henry I stood by old custom, Anselm went once more into exile and ultimately a compromise was arranged on the matter of investiture: elections were to be free, but to take place in the royal chapel; there was to be no investiture before consecration, but feudal homage was permitted. Henry I, indeed, though ostensibly giving freedom to the Church, retained the wardship of sees, allowed no appeals to Rome without permission; no entry of papal bulls, no excommunication of tenants-in-chief, and the right of choosing obedience in the event of a papal schism. In the event, he virtually controlled elections, though at least one legate was allowed to hold a council, and an archbishop of Canterbury was permitted to be *ex officio* legate.

Taking all for all, therefore, Henry I with some success maintained the *status quo*. But during his reign the two allied floods—the one of canon law and papal action, the other of the reformed religious orders—were flowing strongly across the Channel. The Conqueror's ring-fence was breached in many places and each new generation of monks and bishops contained a higher proportion of those brought up in a climate of Gregorian thought and law, that is, brought up to be familiar with a centralised, active, hierarchical clerical body, using and developing a comprehensive body of canon law, and laying down principles and sanctions backed by able popes in alliance with fervent Cluniacs or Cistercians who as bishops or abbots were spreading the new outlook throughout Europe.

Henry I was a strong and efficient ruler whose title was un-assailed. His successor Stephen had a doubtful title and lacked much of Henry's strength and political ability. Recent analysis of his reign has shown that on and off in the turmoil of his reign Stephen attempted to follow old customs, but he had depended upon the pope for recognition as king and the freedom he had promised to the Church was expressed less vaguely than that of his predecessor. He specifically allowed freedom of election, abolition of *regalia* and freedom to receive and obey papal com-mands. Legates were admitted, and the two leading bishops, Henry of Winchester, Stephen's brother, and Theobald of Canterbury, late abbot of Bec, belonged in their different ways to the party of papal allegiance. Meanwhile, the religious orders, new and old, and many individual churches applied for protection and confirmation to Rome, and a multitude of papal charters and letters of protection entered England. The new monasticism had its saints, such as Ailred of Rievaulx, Waltheof of Melrose, Robert of Newminster among the Cistercians and Gilbert of Sempringham, the father of a family of nunneries. All these looked to Rome for approval and support, and such leaders as Bernard of Clairvaux and St Norbert of Prémontré formed a powerful link between the hierarchic and the charismatic elements in church life.

All these forces were responsible for what has seemed para-doxical to some English historians, the great spread of piety and discipline during the politically chaotic reign of Stephen. As a recent historian of his reign has remarked: 'There could be no doubt that the doctrines of high papalism had taken root in England, and that the authority of the church was greater than it ever had been.'[1] At the same time, old customs died hard and were often replaced by methods not strictly canonical. While political and religious motives threw down barriers between England and the pope, and both Henry of Winchester and Theobald used their position as legate freely, both Stephen and the empress used the old regal powers when opportunity offered. Thus in the Durham election of 1143 the empress was prepared to invest her candidate with staff and ring instead of allowing a

1. R. H. C. Davis, *King Stephen*, London 1967, 127.

free election,[1] and in 1141 she settled the appointment on Robert de Sigillo at London.[2] Similarly Stephen when able to do so took bishoprics into his hand until he allowed an election. Theobald for his part, especially when legate, used all his influence to favour his candidates, though his biographer notes that freedom of election by the chapter became more common than before when the archbishop gained power with the withdrawal of Henry of Winchester.[3] But if freedom of the Church implied the functioning of fully canonical procedure, it cannot be said to have obtained entirely in Stephen's reign. It was, indeed, an unobtainable end. The interested powers were so strong, and the openings for intrigue and even simony so large, that a free capitular election could be practicable only when at least one of the two major interested parties—pope and king—had the will and power to hold the ring and allow freedom.

During the six years of life that remained to Theobald after the coronation of Henry II his influence was considerable, perhaps greater than the ailing and saddened archbishop recognised, but the intentions of the young king to recover the powers of his ancestors were clear. Henry was ready, as in the cases of Battle, St Albans and St Augustine's, Canterbury, to try and to decide questions of ecclesiastical jurisdiction without reference to Rome. He hindered appeals to Rome, he reintroduced regalian rights over vacant sees, he taxed the church and he asserted his right to try criminous clerks. Such incidents, and the personality of the king, were clear indications both to the archbishop and to Thomas the chancellor, of the course Henry was setting. It was a collision course between the royal power, oblivious of the change of climate in the Church, and the strength of the Church, based upon the traditional papacy and increased by the expansion of the new canon law with its centralising influence.

Nevertheless, what might have seemed to be a forlorn hope for kings in the aftermath of Canossa and Worms, and in the age of Bernard and Gratian, was made possible by events on the continent of Europe. The papacy was temporarily handicapped by the schism that occurrred after the death of Hadrian IV in 1157. The candidate with the strongest case was undoubtedly Alexander III,

1. *Ibid.*, 61.
2. A. Saltman, *Theobald Archbishop of Canterbury*, London 1956, 95–6.
3. A. Saltman, 125.

a distinguished canonist and diplomat who had been by the side of the late pope in his clash with Frederick Barbarossa, but he had against him the whole of Germany, controlled by the ablest politician, and the firmest and most resilient ruler of his age. Frederick I had been preceded by two emperors, Lothair and Conrad III, who had allowed the Church in Germany to follow papal ways, but he himself consistently traversed Gregorian principles by appointing bishops and extracting the *spolia* and *regalia* at vacancies. Henry II would have been well informed of this by his mother, the late empress, and the example of Rainald of Dassel, raised from the chancellorship (1156) to the archbishopric of Cologne (1159) may well have helped Henry to his decision for Canterbury. In France also Louis VII, often represented as gentle, pious and gullible, succeeded by constant endeavour in restoring the royal influence in episcopal elections and the *regalia* to the *status quo* of forty years earlier.[1] Thus the policy of Henry II followed the pattern of Germany and France, though more ruthlessly pressed home, and he was assisted by the unfortunate position of Alexander III, who could not afford to forfeit the support of a king who controlled so large a part of western Europe.

(iii) Thomas's Episcopal Colleagues

Thomas of London was consecrated archbishop in the presence of all his existing episcopal colleagues. They were men whom he must have met and known well in the king's council and in his duties and travels as chancellor. Their relations with him in the past can scarcely have been intimate or even friendly, save for those who had known him well when he was in the archbishop's household. Much would depend upon their attitude to their new metropolitan.

They were, as has been generally recognised, a notable group of men,[2] and it would not be easy to assemble, at any moment of the middle ages, a bench (if the anachronism be allowed) consisting of a greater variety of types, or a greater proportion of striking personalities. As archbishop Thomas consecrated only two colleagues in his brief term of rule in England, the group

1. This is fully brought out by M. Pacaut, *Alexandre III*, Paris 1956.
2. For a review of the whole group, see *EC.*, chaps. i and ii.

went with him through the controversy to the end; only five died during this period, and three of these were among the oldest and least distinguished. As a group, they were unusually long-lived: Roger of York ruled for 27 years; Hugh of Durham for 42; Bartholomew of Exeter and Richard of Lichfield for 24 and 21 respectively; Nigel of Ely for 33; Gilbert of Hereford and London for 39; Walter of Rochester for 34; Jocelin of Salisbury for 43; and Henry of Winchester for 42. What is, perhaps, even more surprising is that, with the exception of the two survivors from the reign of Henry I, Nigel of Ely and Henry of Winchester, all the others had been elected by some sort of canonical process, if we include Hilary of Chichester, appointed by the pope, and Walter of Rochester, a see traditionally in the gift of the archbishop of Canterbury. The fifteen bishops can be considered in four groups; the royal officials; clerks who had gone up the ladder of preferment; clerks who had risen to distinction outside England; and the monks.

The first class, fairly numerous before and after this period, is here represented by one only, Nigel of Ely, though the archbishop himself was another eminent example. Nigel, an administrator of genius whose son, Richard FitzNeal, inherited his gifts and celebrated them in his classic handbook the *Dialogue of the Exchequer*, was an old man with a chequered and warlike past in 1162, and died in 1169. The second class, that of clerical careerists, contains the bishops of Durham, Lichfield (Coventry), Lincoln, Rochester, Salisbury and Worcester. We have already met Roger of York as a rival of Thomas in Theobald's household. The unanimous condemnation by all the biographers of Thomas, and the harsh verdict of the archbishop himself—'the leader and inspiration of all the evil' [1]—have obscured the picture, but Roger remains an unattractive figure, wealthy, ambitious and un-spiritual. We cannot help wondering why Theobald pressed him upon the York chapter; if he hoped that he would oppose the king's policies or be subordinate he was mistaken. Hugh of

1. 'Totius malitiae ejus incentor', 'Totius hujus discordiae incentor' (*MB.*, vii. (538, 536), 29, 129). These however are examples of the archbishop's milder mood; for a livelier judgement cf. 'ut antiChristi membra tractate' (the reference is to Geoffrey Ridel and Foliot, *MB.*, vii. (587), 131; 'illo infelicissimo Juda, velut putridissimo membro amputato', vii. (536), 14; 'Achitofel in abscondito et Golias in aperto', vii. (537), 18.

Durham, a nephew of Henry of Winchester, was another magnificent, wealthy and litigious prelate, but for some reason that does not appear, he was absent from the scene during the heat of the controversy in 1163–4. Richard Peche of Lichfield was a son of a previous holder of the see, and a man of no distinction. Robert of Lincoln, a member of the Norman family of Chesney and uncle to Gilbert Foliot, seems to have been a man of no strong personality. Jocelin de Bohun, bishop of Salisbury, was another member of the Norman baronage and another protégé of Henry of Winchester. Alexander III writes of him surprisingly as a dear friend of olden days[1] and his son, Reginald the Lombard, was presumably born in Italy, possibly before his father's ordination.[2] Later the friend of Gilbert Foliot, he pursued a devious course in the controversy, ending up in an alliance with Foliot. Walter of Rochester, brother of Theobald, was a colourless personality. Roger of Worcester was a son of Robert, earl of Gloucester, an illegitimate son of Henry I, and was brought up for a time with Prince Henry, later king. He was a man of parts, and had studied at Paris under Robert of Melun the Englishman. Despite his close relations with Henry II he was the most consistent supporter of archbishop Thomas of all his colleagues, and perhaps also the most spiritual. According to Gerald of Wales, Alexander III linked him with Bartholomew of Exeter as the two great luminaries of the English Church.[3]

The third class, that of those who had risen to distinction outside England, has three members, Hilary of Chichester, Bartholomew of Exeter, and Robert of Hereford. All these, in their different ways, were men of the new outlook in church affairs. Hilary of Chichester began his career as a clerk in the household of Henry of Winchester, and in some way of which there is no record entered the service of the Curia and held a distinguished position as counsel and advocate. He was King Stephen's candidate for the archbishopric of York after the deposition of archbishop William in 1147, but the efforts of the Cistercians procured the appointment by Pope Eugenius III of Henry Murdac, abbot of Fountains. Nevertheless, a few days later the pope appointed Hilary to Chichester. There, he was

1. *MB.*, vi. (493), 568.
2. For a discussion of this, see *EC.*, 19; *GF.*, 56 and n.
3. Giraldus Cambrensis, *Opera Omnia*, RS., vii. 57.

active in organising the administration in the new canonical pattern, and was active also in establishing his rights in the diocese, coming into collision, as we have seen, with the abbot of Battle and ultimately with the king.[1] In all the many incidents in which he figures, Hilary 'appears as an extremely quick-witted, efficient, self-confident, voluble man, fully acquainted with the new canon law and with papal claims.'[2] He was extremely tactless, but extremely resilient, and others were prepared to let him speak first even after having experienced the risks that this entailed. He could be very discourteous when he was on the winning side, but was both too able and too pliant to be disregarded.

Bartholomew of Exeter was a man of great distinction and high repute.[3] He was a Norman, and had been a master at Paris, and came to England to hold a post for a short time in Theobald's household. It was probably then that he made the acquaintance of Thomas and formed a friendship with John of Salisbury. When Exeter fell vacant in 1160 Theobald and his secretary, John of Salisbury, made persistent efforts to secure the office for Bartholomew, and were ultimately successful. He was a trained theologian and canonist, and in his later years was frequently employed as judge-delegate by the papacy. He was a man of deliberation and diplomacy rather than of enthusiasm, but he held firmly to his principles as a loyal churchman and retained the respect of both John and archbishop Thomas. Robert of Hereford stands apart from all his colleagues in intellectual distinction. An Englishman by birth, he went to France as did all who had ambitions of what we should now call an academic kind, and was pupil of Hugh of St Victor and Abelard. He then settled at Melun, now an outskirt suburb of Paris, and became himself a celebrated teacher, having among his pupils John of Salisbury, Thomas of London, and Roger of Worcester. His *Liber Sententiarum*, celebrated in its day, is regarded by historians of theology as the last stage in the growth of systematisation that reached its summit with the *Book of the*

1. Cf. pp. 44–5 above.
2. The words quoted are from *EC.*, 27. Since they were written, H. Mayr-Harting has studied Hilary's activities in an article 'Hilary, Bishop of Chichester (1147–69), and Henry II', in *EHR.*, lxxviii. (April, 1963), 209–224, and in *Acta of the Bishops of Chichester*, 1075–1207 (Canterbury & York Society), 1964.
3. For him see A. Morey, *Bartholomew of Exeter*, Cambridge 1937.

Sentences of Peter Lombard, a friend of Robert. He owed his appointment to Hereford to archbishop Thomas, who consecrated him, but for reasons which cannot be known was considerably less warm in his support of the archbishop than his friends would have wished, and he died early in 1167 after little more than three years at Hereford.

The fourth class, that of the monks, contains four names Robert of Bath and Wells, originally a Cluniac of Lewes and later administrator of Glastonbury, was an old man when the great controversy began and does not appear at all in the literature of the struggle. William of Norwich, cathedral prior of that church, was likewise an old man, and seems to have been regarded with reverence and affection by all his colleagues who had dealings with him. He was a steady ally of the archbishop, but either years or temperament kept him from taking part in the later stages of the quarrel.

There remain the two most remarkable personalities among the bishops, Henry of Winchester and Gilbert Foliot of Hereford and London. Both of them have found biographers,[1] and almost all historians of the period have devoted a considerable space to their actions and characters. Moreover, we have ample material for our judgment in the views of contemporaries, for both men came into contact with most of the celebrities of their age, popes, kings, saints and scholars. Henry of Winchester, brother of King Stephen, was an elderly man in 1162 with a life of sound and fury behind him. No longer at the centre of action or intrigue, he allowed a more wise and devout aspect of his personality to emerge, and he appears as an elder statesman, still influential and respected, who stands by the letter and spirit of the reformed church, in contrast to the earlier days in which he had exploited high office and high connections for personal or dynastic ends. Though a close relative of Henry II, and an aristocrat by birth and disposition, he appears as a firm, if not a strident, advocate and friend of a man who, so one would think, had few of the qualities that would appeal to Henry of Blois, the man whom a recent historian has called 'the real grandson of the Conqueror'.[2]

1. Lena Voss, *Heinrich von Blois*, Berlin 1932; A. Morey and C. N. L. Brooke, *Gilbert Foliot and his Letters*, Cambridge 1965, and its companion volume *The Letters and Charters of Gilbert Foliot*, Cambridge 1967.
2. R. H. C. Davis, *King Stephen*, London 1967, 127. But Henry lacked

The last, and by far the most enigmatic figure of all, is that of Gilbert Foliot. Member of a large Norman clan whose scions are found in several counties, and whose name still appears on the map of rural England, Gilbert, who seems to have passed some years in the schools, was probably born in England, but he entered the great abbey of Cluny as a young man and rose very rapidly to be one of the priors of that house, then prior of the dependent Abbeville, then abbot of Gloucester (a post to which family connections seem to have carried him) and then, when little more than thirty, to the see of Hereford in 1148. There he continued to build up a reputation for austere piety and wisdom as a writer and spiritual counsellor to which many references bear witness. When Canterbury fell vacant in 1161 he must certainly have appeared, to himself and to others, an extremely strong candidate, as the most eminent by far of his age-group in the English Church, with the additional recommendation of his monastic status. He would have been unsympathetic to Thomas the Chancellor for almost every reason, spiritual, personal and social, and in fact he was the only one to raise his voice firmly against him in the election meetings. Of his motives, different opinions were held then and since. His almost immediate translation to London, and his nomination by the pope as confessor to Henry II, are evidence of his continued reputation and also, perhaps, of a feeling on the part of authority that some compensation should be made to him for having been passed over in the election to Canterbury. Although archbishop Thomas warmly supported his move to London, Gilbert was clearly a potential, almost an *ex officio*, rival to Thomas in the counsels of the king, and the latent opposition soon became open, and lasted till the death of the archbishop. Throughout the struggle, Foliot was torn by two loyalties, that owing to the king and the feudal structure of English life, and that owing to the hierarchical structure of the Church, and to its head the pope, to whom he was bound both as bishop and as monk. This divided allegiance was in effect an endeavour to serve two, if not three, masters, for Foliot could not rid himself of the bond between himself and his archbishop save by an elaborate construction of

---

both the political sense and the statesmanlike qualities of his grandfather. On the other hand, he was a man of wider appreciations, and mellowed into a dignified and peaceful old age.

F

canonical casuistry. It was to tax both his conscience and his ingenuity for more than six years and to serve, as the underplot serves in Shakespeare's tragedies, to repeat in a minor key the theme that is provided by the predicament of a Lear or an Othello or, as here, of a Thomas Becket.

(iv) Canterbury and York

Among the other cares of the newly consecrated archbishop was the age-old controversy as to rights and mutual relationship between the sees of Canterbury and York. This is not the place to discuss the many complicated and still obscure passages in this vexatious and, in essence, meaningless quarrel, but as it troubled archbishop Thomas from the beginning of his pontificate and was ultimately of crucial importance in the dénouement of his life's drama, a few pages must be devoted to it. It is an essential factor in the fabric of the last year of the story.

The controversy was, so to say, built into English ecclesiastical life from the sixth century by the very author of the revival of that life, Gregory the Great. By solemnly decreeing for England two ecclesiastical provinces, with centres at London and York; by subsequently (though only tacitly) acquiescing in the choice, from existing political conditions, of Canterbury as the southern metropolitan see; by decreeing that in the future precedence should go to the senior by date of consecration, and by giving Augustine a personal commission of surveillance over the whole of Britain, the seeds of confusion and strife were plentifully sown, and bore fruit in season.[1] How far the original choice of London was due to Roman traditions of the sees in England before the Saxon invasions cannot be known with certainty.

The delay in missionary advance to the north, and the retreat from the first Christian settlement at York; the total failure to establish the suffragan sees even when the Celtic and Roman parties merged; the eclipse of the north for more than a century when the invasion of the Northmen came—all these helped to

1. Gregory's instructions are in his letter, given by Bede in his *Ecclesiastical History*, i. 29, (translation in *EHD.*, i. 601). Gregory wrote 'over all the bishops of Britain', presumably referring to the existing Celtic churches.

lessen the prestige of York, while the repeated incursion, by papal authority, of archbishops of Canterbury in the north— first Augustine himself, then Theodore and then Dunstan— greatly enhanced the position of the southern archbishopric, and the absence before the Conquest of regularly settled suffragan sees in the north left the relationship of the two archbishops (when two existed) uncertain. Geographical and historical circumstances had, indeed, helped to create the conception of the archbishop of Canterbury as counseller in chief of the king, and his agent in ecclesiastical matters throughout the kingdom.

When Lanfranc was appointed to Canterbury in 1070 the intention of the Conqueror was undoubtedly to use him as his principal instrument in the reforms of the Church in England. Lanfranc, besides his great administrative ability and wide-ranging view of the Church in the British Isles, had as a part of his programme of organisation, unfamiliar to England, the notion of the office of primate. This, as a joint in the hierarchy between the papacy and the metropolitan, and bearing a certain resemblance to the patriarchates of the east, existed in a few cases, of which Lyons in France and Toledo in Spain were examples, in the days of Gregory the Great, but had not become common in western Europe at that time. It was revived, at least as a theoretical ideal, by the circle of bishops in the ninth century responsible for the false decretals and other unauthentic legislation. Their motive was that which led them to exalt the papacy, viz. to establish a court of appeal against a regional sovereign or a troublesome metropolitan. The office figures in the canonical collections with which Lanfranc was familiar, and was well suited to the self-contained regional Church which William I was establishing in England. Within that Church the primate would have powers of direction and exist as a court of appeal. Implicitly, therefore, rather than explicitly, Lanfranc worked towards embracing the whole of the British Isles under the primacy of Canterbury.

Meanwhile, the papacy was moving towards a more hier-archical and monarchical organization of the Church. In this, the archbishop/metropolitan was the only official in the hierarchy between pope and simple diocesan Ordinary, and his rights were in general limited to the calling and presiding at extraordinary synods, rare metropolitical visitation, and the right of hearing appeals from the courts of his suffragans. At the same time the papacy, by the increasing use of legates with quasi-papal powers, was exercising rights of supervision superior to those of the diocesan or metropolitan, while at the same time the right of appeal to Rome at any stage of a cause was extended and widely used. The function and title of primate were consequently becoming otiose from the papal point of view, while the practice of granting a legateship to an archbishop or even to a bishop was becoming more frequent. Such a legateship, when granted to a prelate with local jurisdiction, was usually valid during the lifetime of the pope who granted it.

These developments help to explain the somewhat tangled interplay of legateship and primacy in the grants made to the two English archbishops during the twelfth century. In particular, 'primacy' became an ambiguous term, implying either a wide superior jurisdiction (such as Lanfranc assumed) or a mere honorific of pre-eminence and precedence. Alexander III acted in terms of the latter type. Archbishop Thomas desired and expected a grant of the former character, implying rights not only of precedence, but of supreme jurisdiction over York. Alexander's grant of the primacy, whether verbally at Tours or later in documents, did not in fact give Thomas the powers he desired, and this may explain his unwillingness to use the title of primate in his letters. In fact, it only occurs once in an authentic instrument in the whole corpus of the three volumes of the Rolls Series.

We cannot follow the reverberations of the conflict between Canterbury and York after 1170, but it may be noted that the ambiguity of title has left a vestigial mark on the titles still held by the archbishop of Canterbury, Primate of All England, and the archbishop of York, Primate of England. A similar pair of titles existed for long in Ireland in the case of the archbishops of Armagh and Dublin.

The see of York was vacant when Lanfranc came to England, and when in 1070 Thomas, a Norman, was appointed to York he was asked to make profession to Lanfranc. Profession of this kind though canonical had fallen into desuetude in the English church.[1] It had spread elsewhere as a quasi-feudal practice and

1. F. Barlow, *The English Church*, 1000–1066, London 1963, 238. 'So careless were the archbishops of Canterbury of their rights that the

was reintroduced in England on the feudal model, but it was also well suited to the Gregorian centralisation of authority and became standard. By this time, however, the sees of both Canterbury and York had immortal watchdogs in the shape of cathedral clergy, soon to be canonical chapters, at York, and the monks of Christ Church at Canterbury. Both these bodies had traditions and some documents which were soon to be augmented by both authentic and forged material, as well as a fund of patriotic partizanship.[1] Thomas of York, instigated by his clergy, refused at first to take the oath to Canterbury, and only yielded with the saving clause that it should set no precedent. At a subsequent council of 1072 the submission of York to Canterbury was confirmed, but York was later encouraged to create an empire of its own by taking the dioceses of Glasgow and St Andrews into its province.

So things stood till 1101, when Gerard was appointed to York by Henry I, and refused to take the oath to Anselm—a refusal which the archbishop took very ill. Both Gerard and Anselm subsequently obtained from the pope confirmation of all past privileges of their sees, some of which were highly dubious,[2] but Pope Paschal II made Gerard promise obedience to Canterbury, and Anselm was empowered as primate to reform the Church in the north.

When Anselm's successor Ralph d'Escures was appointed to Canterbury in 1114 Henry I secured the post of York for his clerk Thurstan. Thurstan, always a robust character, refused to make profession to Canterbury or to be consecrated by the archbishop. By this time the canons of York and the monks of Canterbury had able writers and unscrupulous archivists and a large literature with supporting documents was built up. A period of confusion followed, in which popes gave inconsistent decisions. Ultimately Thurstan was consecrated by the pope,

---

register of professions of faith (sic) made by the bishops to the archbishop before consecration runs only from the end of the eighth century to 870 and, apart from an isolated entry from the mid-tenth century, does not start again till after the Conquest. From York no such register has survived'. Cf. also pp. 303–4.

1. See R. W. Southern, 'The Canterbury Forgeries' in EHR., lxxiii (1958), 193–226.
2. See also the relevant passages in R. W. Southern, St Anselm and his biographer, Cambridge 1963.

Calixtus II, and the declaration of Henry I that the archbishop
of Canterbury was primate of the whole of England, and that all
the bishops of the land were under his jurisdiction had no canonical
effect. Indeed, Calixtus, with the letter of Gregory the Great
before him, built up the position of the archbishop of York.
He was forbidden to make profession to Canterbury and allowed
to be consecrated by his suffragans, if Canterbury refused to act.
One of the motives of Thurstan in helping the creation of the
see of Carlisle was to provide a second bishop (with Durham)
for this eventuality. The next archbishop of Canterbury failed
to obtain Thurstan's profession, but by becoming primate he
acquired a personal ascendancy. Nevertheless, Honorius II gave
Thurstan the right to carry his cross in the southern province,
and to crown the king, but it is most probable that this privilege
referred to the seasonal crown-wearing, not to the original
coronation, which had long been the perquisite of Canterbury.[1]
Thurstan had, thus, succeeded in placing his see on a near-
equality with Canterbury and subsequent popes continued this
policy. Both Innocent II and Eugenius III renewed the prohibition of profession to Canterbury, and precedence was to go
by seniority, as established by Gregory I. Meanwhile the centralising policy of the Gregorian reform favoured legates, who were
appointed by the pope and could be discontinued, rather than
primates, who to some extent derogated from papal powers,
and from 1140 onwards the difficulties of archbishop William
and Henry Murdac in their diocese kept them inactive in the
matter of privilege. Theobald, on the other hand, was given both
primacy and legateship.

When Henry Murdac died in 1153, Theobald secured the
election of his clerk and archdeacon, Roger of Pont l'Evêque.
This may seem a strange choice in view of his jealous and
ambitious behaviour as recorded in the biographies of Thomas,

1. The crown-wearing at Christmas, Easter and Pentecost was a function
of great significance in the reigns of William I and his sons. It was
accompanied by the singing of the *Laudes* (*Christus vincit*, etc.) by the
clerks of the royal chapel under the direction of the chancellor. It has
been held that Henry II allowed the custom to lapse after his early
years, but this might well be accounted for by his absence from England.
William FitzStephen (*MB.*, iii. 83) notes that when archbishop Thomas
was in conflict with the king, the acclamation for the archbishop was
omitted from the *Laudes*.

but besides the conventional duty of a patron to his clients
Theobald may have thought that energy and a certain toughness
were needful qualities for one who had to deal with both Henry
and the redoubtable bishop of Durham, Hugh du Puiset. He may
also have thought that a former archdeacon of Canterbury would
respect that church's claims.

Roger was not one to refrain from bettering his position in
every way possible. He could claim precedence in virtue of
seniority over any future archbishop of Canterbury, though
here the papal acknowledgement of the primacy, or any subsequent
legateship, would give the *pas* to Canterbury. When a vacancy
occurred on Theobald's death, Roger endeavoured to take out
insurance by obtaining permission to carry his cross and crown
kings as granted by previous popes, and in 1161 Henry obtained
for Roger permission to crown his son—a permission which
was not used at the time, but was produced nine years later.[1]
When the vacancy at Canterbury was filled an old rivalry between
colleagues was added to the ancient rivalry of sees, and in May
1163, the matter came up at the council of Tours, where Thomas
was placed on the pope's right hand, but the decision was postponed without prejudice. Subsequently, Roger paraded his
cross at his attendances in the south of England; Thomas protested,
and his protest was supported by Gilbert Foliot.[2] Accordingly,
Alexander in or before January 1164, cancelled his earlier letter
of 1161 and put restraint upon Roger pending a formal settlement.[3]
He wrote at the same time to Thomas explaining that the earlier
letter to Roger had been a mistake due to forgetfulness of previous
papal letters.[4] His circumstances in the years after his election
might well have been his excuse. A month later, when the king's

1. In the letter *Quantum per carissimum* (*MB.*, vi. (310), 206–7). The
dating clause of this letter restricts it to 1167 or 1161. I agree fully with
Miss Anne Heslin (Mrs C. Duggan) that 1161 is almost certainly the
date of this letter. Cf. her article 'The Coronation of the Young King
in 1170' in *Studies in Church History*, ii. 169–78. No proposal to crown
the young Henry was made in 1167, while in 1161 it was certainly on
the tapis; cf. E. Grim, *MB.*, ii. 366, where the imminent coronation
is said to be one of the reasons for the mission of chancellor Thomas to
England early in 1162.
2. *MB.*, v. (27–8), 44–7; *GFL*, no. 146.
3. *MB.*, v. (41–2), 67–8.
4. *MB.*, v. (43), 69.

favour had been lost irretrievably by Thomas, Henry, while pressing the pope for confirmation of the Constitutions of Clarendon, added a request that a legateship should be conferred on Roger of York. This the pope, in the interests of peace, agreed to do, but he accompanied his concession with an oath to be taken by Henry that he would not use the papal instrument without further express permission. Henry, therefore, in disgust returned the letter unused.[1] In the same year the primacy was promised verbally to Thomas at Sens.[2] Two years later (5 April 1166) the pope forbade the coronation and anointing of a king of England by anyone save the archbishop of Canterbury, confirmed the primacy to Thomas with its traditional rights, and finally bestowed the legateship (24 April 1166).[3] The primacy and legateship were later suspended by the various legations appointed to negotiate between the king and the archbishop, and though the legateship was restored after the failure of the mission of Vivian and Gratian, Thomas did not receive powers over the whole of England till 1170. In 1170 he forbade any coronation by his suffragans and the bishop of Durham in virtue of his powers as legate. Roger of York was forbidden directly by the pope.[4] But this is to anticipate events.

1. *MB.*, v. (50–1), 85–8; (53), 91.
2. *MB.*, vi. (315), 215.
3. *MB.*, v. (169, 170, 172–3), 323, 324–6, 328–31.
4. *MB.*, vii. (633, 648), 217, 256–7.

CHAPTER 6

Controversy and Councils, 1163-64

(i) Criminous Clerks

Soon after his consecration, and greatly to the king's surprise and indignation, Thomas resigned the chancellorship. The action was inevitable if the archbishop was to have any freedom of action, but it was inevitably also an 'unfriendly act' from Henry's point of view, for it brought to an abrupt end a brilliant partnership of eight years.[1] No successor was appointed for the time being. Thomas continued to be the first signatory of charters as archbishop, as he had been as chancellor, and it was not till early in 1163 that Geoffrey Ridel appeared as first witness, though he was apparently never styled chancellor.[2] In the fullest sense of the word, Thomas never had a successor in the chancery. He was less willing to abandon the archdeaconry of Canterbury, and it was only at the king's insistent request that he did so. Henry filled the vacancy with Geoffrey Ridel. The reason for Thomas's unwillingness is not clear, but it is probably significant that Ridel, like Becket, held both posts, and Thomas may have been apprehensive of the damage that would be done in the archdiocese by *archidiabolus noster*.[3]

One of the first acts of a newly installed bishop or abbot in the middle ages was to consider the losses his estates might have incurred through the weakness or misfortune of his predecessor. For what had happened in the vacancy, Thomas himself was responsible. Three losses in particular caught his eye. One was Rochester castle, probably occupied by a party during the troubles

1. William of Canterbury, *MB.*, i. 12.
2. *Handbook of British Chronology*, 2 ed. Powicke and Fryde, 82. R. W. Eyton, *Court, Household and Itinerary of Henry II*, London 1878, 60. (? March, 1163).
3. The words are cited as from John of Salisbury by Robertson (*MB.*, vi. 300 n. 3).

of Stephen's reign; another was the failure of the earl of Clare to do homage for Tonbridge castle; a third was a fief in Eynsford, seized during the vacancy by William de Ros. The last-named gave most trouble, and was excommunicated by the archbishop. This roused the king, who claimed that a tenant-in-chief should not be excommunicated without royal permission. The archbishop yielded *ex gratia*, and had no thanks for so doing. This, however, was in the summer of 1163, and hitherto the friendship of Henry and Thomas had to all appearances remained unchanged. Previously, in January, Henry had returned to England after an absence of more than four years. Archbishop Thomas, with his ward the young prince Henry, met him at Southampton and the two embraced and talked together alone during several days.[1] Subsequently, the archbishop was with the king at intervals and at the Council till the end of March. This was, perhaps, the last period during which they met as friends, and their association was still firm enough to silence the detractors of the archbishop at court.

At about that time a move took place that was to be pregnant with consequence. The bishop of London, Richard of Belmeis II, had died after a long period of illness in May 1162. Gilbert Foliot, bishop of Hereford and his cousin, had been asked to administer the finances during his illness and had refused; consequently, Becket as chancellor had farmed the see. Now, early in 1163 the king, supported by archbishop Thomas, had petitioned the pope for the translation of Foliot to London. The ostensible reason given was that Henry had chosen Gilbert Foliot as his spiritual director, and that he would be more easily at hand in London. The letter of Alexander III, allowing the translation and approving the relationship of bishop and king, was followed up by two from archbishop Thomas, the first praising Gilbert's merits, the second extolling the close alliance between the sees of London and Canterbury and expressing the pleasure it would give to the writer to have Gilbert near for counsel.[2] The whole affair raises questions for the historian that cannot be answered. How far was Thomas then aware of Gilbert's obstinate objection to his election twelve months

1. H. Bosham, *MB.*, iii. 252.
2. The four letters are in *MB.*, v. (16–19), 24–30.   *GFL.*, nos. 143, 142, 141, 144.

previously? If this was public knowledge could he have written so blandly? And why was the invitation not sent to Gilbert till a year after the vacancy occurred? Was it a move of counter-insurance on the part of the king? Or a generous offer of a consolation-prize by Thomas? We must remember (what the letters tell us) that hitherto the amity of king and archbishop was externally firm, and it would certainly be mistaken to regard Thomas's letters as hypocrisy. He had won the first round and could afford to be generous, and he had not yet heard that Foliot had refused to promise obedience to Canterbury.

Shortly after this the archbishops of Canterbury and York were present with the king's permission at the Council of Tours (19–21 May, 1163). Thomas's progress thither was reminiscent of his visit to Paris some years earlier. The whole population of the city and the council itself, save for the pope himself and two cardinals, went forth to meet him, and Alexander rose to greet him when he appeared.[1] It was their first meeting. Then, and on his return, all seemed well between him and Henry, though the archbishop had remonstrated with the king for keeping Worcester vacant since 1160. In any case, two bishops were elected this year, Roger of Worcester in March and Robert of Hereford in December or earlier; both were consecrated by Thomas. In this year also, two notable ceremonies took place; the consecration of Reading Abbey, the foundation and burial place of Henry I, and the translation of Edward the Confessor at Westminster.

The biographers agree that the first open clash between Henry and Thomas took place at Woodstock, where the king was staying 1–7 July, over the customary gratuitous payment by the shires to the sheriffs of two shillings per hide for courteous behaviour. These the king proposed to standardise on the rolls of the exchequer. When all others acquiesced, the archbishop stood out, arguing that in this way all control over the sheriffs would be lost as they would have no inducement to be reasonable. Thomas's stand, like that of Hampden five centuries later, was a striking act of courage against royal autocracy, and he won the day. A few days later, another controversy arose. Philip de Brois, a canon of Lincoln, had been accused of killing a knight, and had purged himself at the spiritual court of Lincoln. He

1. H. Bosham, *MB.*, iii. 254–5.

was subsequently threatened with further proceedings by his enemy Simon FitzPeter, recently a justice in eyre in Bedfordshire. Philip gave as good as he had received and the justice brought the matter before the king, who insisted on a new trial. The archbishop agreed to the trial but claimed de Brois as a cleric for his own court. De Brois was acquitted of homicide, but admitted having insulted the royal justice, and was sentenced to a fine of his prebend for two years, to a scourging, and to exile. The king was not satisfied; he had wished for a death sentence. Within a few days came the withdrawal of the excommunication of William of Eynesford.

On 1 October the king held a full council at Westminster; all the bishops and fifty or more barons were present.[1] An anonymous writer states categorically that the purpose of the assembly was to settle the matter of the primacy between Canterbury and York. It may be that the proceedings were in part a synod. In any case, the latent anger of the king broke out suddenly over the question of clerical immunity. This matter, though not the root cause of the great quarrel that followed, was in a sense its diamond point. It must, therefore, be set out as clearly as possible. Like more than one of the debated issues of the twelfth century, clerical immunity had its roots in the distant past, and only by a recognition of this can we hope to reach a clear understanding of the problem. A merely pragmatic judgment, based on the principles of commonsense administrative reform, will be inadequate, as will also a merely emotional judgment which strangely enough, with historians of the past hundred years, takes the form of indignation that clerics should escape the harsh and barbarous punishments that were so lightly imposed by the governments of the age. Rather than this, we have to discover what was the ancient canonical doctrine and the subsequent practice in the western Church. We shall find that, here as elsewhere, the matter was rendered more intractable by a misunderstanding of the conditions under which the earliest legislation had been framed, and also by the difficulties caused by the unauthentic legislation put out by the forgers of the ninth century.[2]

1. For a detailed account of the proceedings at Westminster, Clarendon and Northampton see *EC.*, chap. iii, 53–90.
2. A good brief selection of the evidence on this issue is in *EHD.*, ii.

In the first three centuries of Christianity the Church, within ts own ambit, imposed its own set of penalties and excommunications, while for social and other criminal actions Christians, whether clerical or lay, were amenable to the imperial law. The Christian Empire, when it came, recognised the clerical status and its hierarchical constitution, but in general left the trial and punishment of criminous clerks to the bishop. When the law was codified under Justinian I there was a conflict of doctrine. One law laid down that in civil cases the ordinary court should deal with clerics, while in criminal cases the provincial prefect should have jurisdiction. If found guilty in the latter case, the clerk was to be degraded by the bishop and then suffer the legal penalty.[1] Another law, however, gave the following procedure. A cleric accused to the bishop and adjudged guilty was to be degraded and handed over for trial and punishment to the secular judge. If the accusation was first laid before a secular judge and established, the bishop was to review the case and if satisfied, to degrade the clerk and hand him over; if not satisfied, appeal to the emperor was allowed.[2] Thus in both cases the bishop was an essential actor, and in the second the bishop's decision or acceptance of a decision was mandatory. In no case did privilege exist for a condemned criminal, who suffered the normal punishment. Bishops, on the other hand, could not be brought before a lay court; they were tried by their equals.

In the western Church in the seventh and eighth centuries there were differences of practice.[3] The *privilegium fori* was accepted only for bishops, not for clerks as such, but gradually they were equated with bishops, and an ecclesiastical trial was mandatory before the culprit was handed over for punishment. But there was no universal law or practice. In some regions,

---

12–22; a fuller treatment is in R. Foreville, *L'Eglise et la Royauté en Angleterre, 1154–89*, Paris 1943, 136 ff. In what follows in the text I have been greatly enlightened by Dr C. Duggan's article, 'The Becket Dispute and the Criminous Clerks', in *Bulletin of the Institute of Historical Research*, xxxv, no. 91 (May 1962), 1–28. In his note on pp. 2–3 Duggan gives a survey of the literature on the subject.

1. Novella lxxxiii. For text and reff. see C. Duggan, 26.

2. Novella cxxiii. *Ibid.*

3. R. Génestal, *Le Privilegium Fori en France*, 2 vols., Paris 1921–24. This work is disappointingly meagre on Merovingian and Carolingian practice.

of which England was one, the absence of a single ruler gave the
bishops the power and responsibility of dealing with offenders
themselves.[1] Elsewhere a secular trial was followed sometimes
by degradation, sometimes by the penalty incurred by seculars
for a similar offence, but most often by confinement in a monastery.
The situation was changed and, as elsewhere, confused by the
forged decretals and capitularies of the ninth century. These
in general conflated the imperial law of the Theodosian and
Justinian codes with decrees of councils, and they were followed
in different ways by the canonists of the eleventh and early
twelfth centuries. The matter was particularly confused by the
persistence with which the forgers had recourse to canons dealing
with clerics in revolt against their bishop, in which case recourse
had been allowed to the secular power when the bishop found
himself unable to cope with the situation. But in general the
canonists kept matters within episcopal control; it was the bishop's
duty and right to try the offence whatever might happen afterwards.[2]

There is scarcely any factual evidence as to the treatment of
criminous clerks, as distinct from merely civil delinquents, in
the Anglo-Saxon Church between the accession of Alfred and
the death of Edward the Confessor. The law however is fairly
clear. In Ethelred's code of 1014 we read:

26. If a priest becomes a homicide or otherwise commits too grave a
    crime, he is then to forfeit both his ecclesiastical orders and his
    country, and to go on pilgrimage as far as the pope may prescribe
    for him. . . .

27. If anywhere a priest takes part in false witness or perjury, or is
    the accessory and accomplice of thieves, he is then to be cast
    out from the fellowship of those in orders, and to forfeit both the
    society and friendship and every dignity. . . .[3]

In the laws of Cnut (1020–23) this appears more briefly, after a
repetition of c. 26:

43. If a man in holy orders commits a capital crime, he is to be
    seized and kept for the bishop's judgement according to the
    nature of the deed.[4]

1. See below, p. 83.   2. C. Duggan, art. cit., 6–10.
3. Ethelred (code VIII) in EHD., i. (46), 412.
4. Law of Cnut, 1020–23. EHD., i. (50), 425 (c. 43; c. 41 repeats viii
Ethelred c. 26).

Benefit of clergy, therefore, existed for grave and very grave crimes; it removed the possibility of a death sentence or of mutilation, but it entailed degradation and the loss of all clerical privileges, with exile and papal penance. How far the last two punishments were applied is quite unknown; some delinquents doubtless vanished from sight in London or one of the other towns; but those who were degraded (unless they sued for and obtained reinstatement) would be liable as laymen for the penalty of any subsequent misdeed. The case would presumably have come up at the shire court, where the bishop was president, and it has been suggested very reasonably[1] that ecclesiastical cases were heard in a kind of committee of the court, meeting perhaps at the bishop's residence. If this were so, the well-known writ of the Conqueror for the separation of ecclesiastical cases from lay proceedings would have done little more than regularize what was already happening.[2]

There is no reason to suppose that the Conqueror, when acknowledging a spiritual jurisdiction, intended to deprive the Church of its existing privileges, but there is no evidence of what happened to criminous clerks. The sanctions applied by archbishop Thomas in the case of Philip de Brois, would suggest that the procedure outlined in Ethelred's law was still the theoretical norm, but rarely followed in practice.[3] Its application was Thomas's reply to the cry that clerks escaped scot-free. But from the days of Lanfranc onwards, and still more under Henry I, two warring jurisdictions came into view. The infiltration of canon law gradually introduced the doctrine of the privilege of clergy in its full extent, while the tightening grip of the royal prerogative, increased by the introduction of itinerant royal justices, provided the king with a reasonable grievance. Until these justices learnt of delinquent clerks there had been little chance of public scandal, but the new methods of evidence given by jury showed up the imperfections of the church courts, in which the accused could escape if he obtained a sufficient number of oath-helpers.

Henry II, with the example of his grandfather and the breakdown

1. By F. Barlow, *The English Church*, 1000–1066, London 1963, 149–52.
2. *Ibid.*, 274–6, and D. J. A. Matthew, *The Norman Conquest*, London 1966.
3. H. Bosham, *MB.*, iii. 265–6.

of government under Stephen before his eyes, was resolved to bring the criminous clerk within his net, but he was no longer working, as William I had worked, in what was almost a free field. He now had to face the new canon law, which his own clerical officials knew well in its main lines, but they also had some acquaintance with the civil law,[1] and could thus meet the canonists in a straight fight. On balance, this was probably a disadvantage for the king's cause. A confrontation between reputedly ancient custom and new and questionable canon law might have been an easier task than setting up civil law against the canons.

One further point must be mentioned. In the canons relating to the trial of a cleric the phrase frequently occurs that after degradation a convicted ex-clerk should be 'handed over to the court (*tradatur curiae*)'.[2] This phrase was familiar to the supporters of Henry, and they understood it to mean that the culprit was to be handed over to the royal court of law either to be its servant or to be amenable to any penalty that might seem fitting. Thomas for his part accepted the second interpretation, but applied it to the future status of the delinquent after degradation, when he was no longer indictable or punishable for his past offence, but liable to trial by the secular court for any further crime. In fact, the phrase can be traced back to the Theodosian code and (as Thomas realised) to accounts of the epoch of Constantine.[3] In these it apparently implied a reduction to the state of imperial slavery, but the phrase was ambiguous. In some contexts it seems to mean 'to be reduced to civil status' or 'to be put under the jurisdiction of the secular court', or even as Henry's advisers held, 'to be handed over to the king's court'.[4] The archbishop was logically compelled to reject the last meaning, for it would imply that canonists did not accept his oft-repeated axiom that 'God did not punish twice for the same offence'. This he repeated in season and out, so that historians have accepted it as an original coinage. Actually, the words, based on a phrase in Jerome's

1. *MB*. iii. 266–7. 'Rex, quorumdam fretus consilio utriusque juris se habere peritiam ostentantium'.
2. *MB*., iii. 267. See C. Duggan, *art. cit.*, 6–10.
3. H. Bosham, *MB*., iii. 270 and n. 2.
4. *MB*., iii. 267.

commentary on the prophet Nahum,[1] had come down the centuries in canon after canon. Its original application, indeed, was to forbid excommunication subsequent to degradation for a grave crime committed by a cleric, but the canon, which had been taken up by Gratian, could be applied *a fortiori* to a secular penalty subsequent to an ecclesiastical one. Such an application had been made by commentators before or contemporary with Thomas's involvement, and, more appositely still, John of Salisbury, in a work presented to chancellor Becket in 1159, had applied the maxim to criminous clerks.[2] As is well known, it was embodied by Alexander III in the decretal *Licet praeter* (1178) addressed to the archbishop of Salerno, which gave final canonical recognition to the privilege of clergy.[3] It was not, therefore, either an invention of archbishop Thomas or a novel application to a particular situation.

In short, both Henry and the archbishop had colourable canonical opinion behind their respective interpretations and attitudes, but the tide was undoubtedly setting in favour of the clerks, and Gratian's judgment was nearer to that of Thomas than to that of Henry, while Gratian's commentators were to be in favour of Thomas's opinion.[4] If, therefore, we consider the archbishop as a canonist of the papalist allegiance, his interpretation of the canons can be fully justified. If we look to him for wise statesmanship, it may be that we should give another answer.

At the Westminster meeting of 1 October the king brought up the matter of criminous clerks, on which he and his counsellors had prepared their case. On the practical level his arguments had great force. Unless clerks guilty of grave crimes of violence were severely punished, they would multiply. They were not less guilty than lay criminals and degradation would have no deterrent effect. Passing to the canonical issue, the king and his advisers made much of the canon in which it was written that clerical offenders, after condemnation by an ecclesiastical court,

1. Nahum i. 9. See Z. N. Brooke, *The English Church and the Papacy*, Cambridge 1931, 205 n. 1, and C. Duggan, *art. cit.*, 15 ff.
2. *Policraticus*, ed. C. C. J. Webb, Oxofrd 1909, ii. 364. Cited by C. Duggan, *art. cit.*, 17 n. 5.
3. *Corpus Juris Canonici*, ed. Friedberg, ii: Decretales Greg. IX, iii, 1, 4.
4. See texts in C. Duggan, *art. cit.*, 6–8, 18–23.

should be 'handed over to the royal court' for punishment. Relegation to a monastery for penance was scarcely adequate, and to send a man into exile was the king's prerogative, not the bishop's.[1] To this Thomas and his colleagues replied clause by clause, beginning with the Gelasian assertion of the two powers of which the spiritual was the superior, and dwelling on the sacred character of the priesthood. They gave another sense, as has been already noted, to the phrase 'let him be handed over to the royal court', maintaining that this implied that for the future the degraded clerk should be indictable as a layman for subsequent offences. They also claimed the ancient right of bishops to send men out of the realm, or on penitential pilgrimage abroad.[2] Henry, enraged by opposition, cut the argument short by asking if the bishops would undertake to observe the royal customs. Thomas, with the unanimous support of his colleagues, answered that he was willing to do so in so far as might be lawful for a clerk (*salvo ordine suo*). Hilary of Chichester alone stood out and substituted the words 'in good faith' (*bona fide*). This satisfied nobody. The king told him he wanted a plain 'Yes' without conditions, and the archbishop later rounded on Hilary for breaking away from his colleagues. Henry's fatigue and anger had increased during the day's argument, and he parted from the bishops without a word. Next morning he left London before dawn, but before departing he required the archbishop to give up the castles and estates of which he had retained custody even after ceasing to be chancellor. Many of the bishops, thoroughly alarmed, followed the king for further talk, and blamed Thomas for his stand.[3]

At this time Pope Alexander III was at Sens, and news of the trouble soon reached him.[4] He urged moderation, and sent Robert of Melun, formerly Thomas's master, and Philip, abbot of L'Aumône and sometime prior of St Bernard at Clairvaux, to persuade the archbishop to submit. The king, they were instructed to say, was insistent merely to save his face before his barons. He would not abuse any accommodation that was made.

1. H. Bosham, *MB.*, iii. 267.
2. *MB.*, iii. 270.
3. *MB.*, iii. 273 ff.
4. Henry applied to the pope for confirmation of the Constitutions before the council of Northampton, *MB.*, v. (50), 86.

The archbishop at last allowed himself to be persuaded; he sought out the king at Oxford, and agreed to accept the ancestral customs in good faith.[1] He lacked still the inner strength to stand firm, and he displayed once more that lack of political or social judgment that was to do harm to his cause on more than one occasion: he changed direction suddenly without warning or seeking to persuade his colleagues. Having given way, he found Henry, egoist as he was, profoundly ungrateful. The archbishop had insulted the king, and must now undo the insult. Let him call his colleagues together: the king would call his barons, and all should hear the archbishop's recantation.[2]

(ii) Clarendon

Such was the genesis of the celebrated meeting at Clarendon, the wooden hunting-lodge not far from Salisbury, destined more than once to give its name to men and events of note in English history, but until recently not to be found upon the map of Wiltshire.[3] The meeting took place on 13 January 1164. The two parties were apparently separated at first; the king, his barons and officials in one hall or chamber, the archbishop and his colleagues in another. Thomas remained silent; he had already repented of his surrender at Oxford. The bishops also, it seems, had repented of their weakness at Westminster. Consequently, they presented an unbroken front, the only absentees being Roger of York, Hugh of Durham and William of Norwich. The accounts of the biographers, to which can be added a version of the story by Gilbert Foliot,[4] are difficult to harmonize, but a picture similar to that of Westminster can be seen in glimpses. Thomas and the bishops stood firm even in face of the fury of

1. William of Canterbury, *MB.*, i. 15.
2. H. Bosham, *MB.*, iii. 276–8.
3. The site of Clarendon was partially excavated more than thirty years ago, see 'Clarendon Palace: An interim Report', by Tancred Borenius and John Charlton, in *Antiquaries' Journal*, xvi. (1936), 55–84. See also R. A. Brown and H. M. Colvin in *The History of the King's Works*, ed. H. M. Colvin, London 1963, ii. 910–18.
4. Gilbert's account is in his letter *Multiplicem, MB.*, v. (225), 527–9; *GFL.*, pp. 239 ff.

the king—'as is the roaring of a lion, so is the fury of a king'—and the threats of the barons, who at one point broke in upon the bishops threatening violence. Here, as later at Northampton, there seems to be a degree of frustration and pantomime in the barons' actions, and even in the king's. In the last resort, they were men of faith and feared the Church and her sanctions. The ministers of a later Henry could afford to proceed more calmly: to them *praemunire* was more real than excommunication.

Pleas were more effective than threats. The bishops, two earls and two Templars in turn plied the archbishop. The Templars were Richard of Hastings, Master of the English Templars, and another well known at court, and the earls Robert of Leicester and Reginald of Cornwall. There is some discrepancy about the bishops, but Jocelin of Salisbury, and William of Norwich seem the most likely, as both of them were out of favour with Henry. In any case, whether from fear of the consequences to himself and his allies, or from concern for the fate of particular bishops, Thomas at last gave way—once again with a sudden tack off course without consulting or informing his colleagues.[1] He told the king, who immediately bade him to command his fellow-bishops to follow his lead. They did so, and the king immediately ordered the barons and clerks of the chancery to set down the customs in writing. Herbert of Bosham explicitly asserts that neither the king, as young, nor the archbishop, as a recent appointment, had any conception of a complete list of customs. This seems scarcely credible, as Henry had been king for nine years, during which Thomas had been his chief executive minister, but it must probably be taken to mean, at the very least, that no list of customs existed.[2] Whether Henry was wise in ordering a list to be put in writing is another matter.

The Constitutions of Clarendon, as presented to the bishops, were given under sixteen headings. Many of these concerned matters affecting the Church, but in no sense controversial, such as the last, that sons of villeins ought not to be ordained without the consent of the lord on whose lands they were known to have

1. W. FitzStephen, *MB.*, iii. 48.
2. H. Bosham, *MB.*, iii. 280. 'Nec enim rex, qui adhuc juvenis, sicut nec archipraesul suus novus, pristinas regni consuetudines nisi ex aliorum relatu cognoscebat.' An extraordinary statement: Henry had been king nine years during which Thomas had been chancellor for eight.

been born. There were, however, six which, in the eyes of church-men, traversed the rights of the Church. They are as follows:[1]

> I. If a dispute shall arise between laymen, or between clerks and laymen, or between clerks, concerning advowson and pre-sentation to churches, let it be treated in the court of the lord king.

This implied that the king considered these to be cases of real property, while the Church held them to concern the cure of souls.

> III. Clerks cited and accused of any matter shall, when summoned by the king's justice, come before the king's court to answer there concerning matters which shall seem to the king's court to be answerable there, but in such a way that the justice of the king shall send to the court of Holy Church to see how the case is there tried. And if the clerk be convicted or shall confess, the Church ought no longer to protect him.

This clause is composed badly and with ambiguity, but the meaning appears to be that the king's justices should issue summonses for all civil offences and when the justices have ascertained that there is a case to be tried on a grave charge, they should send the accused for trial before a spiritual court. There, an emissary from the justices shall observe the proceedings to see that justice is done, and if the clerk is judged guilty, shall receive him after sentence and degradation, and restore him to the king's court for sentence and punishment. We have seen how this con-flicted with the canonical procedure, as understood by the arch-bishop.

> IV. It is not lawful for archbishops, bishops and beneficed clergy to depart from the kingdom without the lord king's leave.

This was aimed at controlling visits to the pope, for whatever purpose.

> VII. No one who holds of the king in chief nor any of the officers of his demesne shall be excommunicated, nor the lands of any one of them placed under interdict, unless application shall first be made to the lord king.
> VIII. With regard to appeals, if they should arise, they should proceed from the archdeacon to the bishop, and from the

1. This follows the version in *EHD.*, ii. 718 ff.

bishop to the archbishop. And if the archbishop should fail
to do justice, the case must finally be brought to the lord
king, in order that by his command the dispute may be
determined in the archbishop's court, in such wise that it may
proceed no further without the assent of the lord king.

This article is aimed at preventing appeals to Rome.[1]

XII. When an archbishopric or bishopric is vacant, or any abbey
or priory of the king's demesne, it ought to be in his own hand,
and he shall receive from it all revenues and profits as part of
his demesne. And when the time has come to provide for the
church, the lord king ought to summon the more important of
the beneficed clergy of the church, and the election ought to
take place in the lord king's chapel with the assent of the lord
king and the advice of the clergy of the realm whom he shall
summon for this purpose. And the clerk elected shall there do
homage and fealty to the lord king as his liege lord for his
life and limbs and his earthly honour, saving his order,
before he is consecrated.

These are the articles to which the archbishop took exception at
once, and they are the ones that a modern historian would select at
sight. Later in the controversy several others were added as
unacceptable, but had the six former not existed, it is unthinkable
that a breach would have occurred between the king and the
Church.

How far was Henry justified in claiming these customs as those
of his grandfather? The first, concerning advowsons, was a point
of legitimate difference, as it concerned the right of presentment,
not the appointment itself. In pre-Conquest days, it would
presumably have been a matter of decision by the shire court;
when the ecclesiastical court was given separate status, it was
probably taken by the royal court as concerning real property.
Later, in 1179, it became the subject of a new possessory assize,
that of *Darrein Presentment*, and a jury decided who was the last
to exercise the right.[2]

1. For another interpretation of this clause see H. G. Richardson and
G. O. Sayles, *The Governance of Medieval England*, Edinburgh 1963,
306–7.
2. For later developments see C. R. Cheney, *From Becket to Langton*,
Manchester 1956.

CLARENDON

The site of Clarendon palace, a few miles east of Salisbury, lies among trees and scrub in a landscape of open country. The photograph shows the plan as revealed by excavation. *Cambridge University Aerial Photography*.

The third clause has already been discussed, and we have seen that in pre-Conquest days criminous clerks were judged and sentenced by the bishop. The royal claim probably began when itinerant justices began to function regularly. Under Stephen the Church claimed full jurisdiction, e.g. in the case of Osbert, the alleged murderer of archbishop William of York.[1]

The fourth clause did not express a pre-Conquest royal claim, but William the Conqueror has asserted it, and he was followed by his sons.

The eighth clause concerned another right asserted by the Conqueror and maintained by his sons, which had been seriously breached under Stephen. Both this and its predecessor were wholly incompatible with the Gregorian conception of the Church, and with the old canon law as now revised and applied.

The twelfth clause asserted two rights, that of the *regalia* and that of the election and appointment of bishops. The claim of the monarch to take into his control and manage the episcopal estates during a vacancy was common in Europe during the eleventh century, and in some cases carried with it the enjoyment by the king of all the revenues of a bishopric, and the superfluous revenues of an abbey after the pension of the monks had been paid. In pre-Conquest England it was common for the king to supervise the estates of a bishop during a vacancy, but they were managed for the benefit of the see.[2] William the Conqueror continued the practice, but the feudalisation of the Church led easily to the assimilation of a bishopric or abbey to the fee of a lay tenant-in-chief, which on the demise of its holder fell back into the hands of the king till it was restored to an heir or bestowed on another. Whether William I began this assimilation is not clear, but William II certainly treated sees and abbeys as feudal fees, and not only enjoyed the revenues, but prolonged the vacancies to his own profit. Henry I carried on the practice, but Stephen was less able to assert his claim. Henry II, as we have seen, renewed the practice, and Thomas as chancellor had greatly profited by it. As practised by the kings from William II onward it was certainly both

---

1. *JS.*, *Ep.* 16; *GFL.*, no. 127.
2. M. Howell, *Regalian Right in Medieval England*, London 1962, 7–8, citing Ordericus Vitalis, ed. le Prevost, iii. 313. Miss Howell's book illustrates the development under the Norman kings.

uncanonical and unjust, particularly when the see was left vacant for purely financial gain.

As regards episcopal election, we have seen that under the Old English monarchy, the choice was made by the king and the Witan, or by the king himself.[1] William the Conqueror continued to appoint, no doubt often on the advice of Lanfranc and others. When the papacy became involved in the investiture contest, Anselm stood out for canonical procedure, but ultimately agreed on a compromise identical with that of Clarendon clause XII. This, though tolerated by the papacy, was not canonical, and during the reign of Stephen some, but not all, of the elections were freely made by the canonical electors, viz. the clergy of the church with local notabilities, monastic and lay. In any controversy, it was natural that the hierarchy should stand out for the full canonical freedom.

Thus it may be said that by and large the royal officials who drew up the Constitutions were justified in declaring that they represented the customs of fifty years earlier, in the reign of Henry I. If past practice were the only criterion, however, archbishop Thomas could have appealed to a still earlier age, that of Edward the Confessor, when the Church was in many ways freer than under the Normans and Angevins. But the real conflict was not between length of tradition, but between two conceptions of the relations of Church and monarchy. If some of the articles, such as that regarding criminous clerks or homage before consecration, may seem to reflect a more realistic outlook than the claims of the papal party, Henry was at least equally unrealistic in attempting to forbid appeals and visits to the pope, and in demanding that the rights of *regalia* in their extreme form should be acknowledged by the Church. These were matters on which an effective papacy, let alone a Gregorian reformist pope, was bound by canon law and traditional practice to claim a right of control. To an independent outside witness, looking on Christian Europe in the age of reform, a fair judgment might have been that regarding advowsons, criminous clerks and homage before appointment, there was room for discussion, or at least for bargaining, while on the other points no surrender would have been possible. On the merely canonical level the papal opposition was bound to be stronger still. Regal custom and canon law were in collision. Henry would have been

1. F. Barlow, *The English Church* 1000–1066, London 1963, 99 ff.

wise to accept a verbal and general assurance, and to use his strong position with tact. By demanding solemn assent to a list of propositions he was asking too much. *Expressa nocent*, remarked Herbert the lawyer more than once[1]. You harm your case by putting it out in set terms, for you lose freedom of manoeuvre. Once seen, the Constitutions were sure to be opposed, and the only course would then have been to negotiate a 'package deal' somewhat on the lines of the final compromise. But neither Henry nor Thomas would have bought a package in 1164.

When the archbishop read the roll of the Constitutions he instantly regretted his previous complaisance. He had been told that appeasement would placate the king; now he was asked to seal away the whole programme of the Gregorian reformation. He accepted his copy of the threefold chirograph, but refused to seal at once and asked for time to consider the matter. He left Clarendon in a mood of deep depression. Within a few days he wrote to the pope begging absolution for his sin of disloyalty. Meanwhile he suspended himself from the service of the altar for forty days, until the rescript came from Sens giving him the papal absolution.[2] Henry, for his part, sent a copy of the Constitutions to Alexander III for approval which, needless to say, they did not obtain in full. The pope allowed six—that is nos. II, VI, XI, XIII and XVI which fell within the normal powers of government—but condemned all those that have been mentioned above, with the addition of four others where there was a clash between royal and ecclesiastical competence and jurisdiction. Nevertheless, Thomas was anxious to confess his fault in person to the pope and twice attempted to cross the Channel, in clear violation of clause IV of Clarendon. Then, in a last attempt to restore good relations with Henry he waited on him at Woodstock, only to be met by a sarcastic query from the king: 'Do you find my kingdom not big enough for both of us?'.[3]

Little is known of the six months that followed, save that Thomas was active in his diocese, and took no notice of the objectionable clauses of the Constitutions.

1. E.g. *MB*., iii. 410. 'Dicebant etenim quod nocerent expressa', and 447. 'Hic enim, ut asserebant universi, nocerent expressa'.
2. *MB*., v. 88–9. E. Grim, ii. 383; *GW*., lines 1031–5.
3. H. Bosham, *MB*., iii. 294. 'Tanquam si ipsos duos simul capere non posset [terra].'

(iii) Northampton

The occasion of the next and critical confrontation was the affair of John the Marshal. This baron, a member of the exchequer staff, claimed land at Mundham that was part of the archiepiscopal manor of Pagham. Recently, so we are told, the king had issued a constitution giving a vassal the right of appeal to his overlord if the latter failed after two days to do him justice in a plea in his court. All that he then needed to do was to swear with two oath-helpers that his case had been unjustly delayed. John the Marshal, wishing to ingratiate himself with Henry, followed the procedure just mentioned, swearing, so his opponents said, upon a troper (a liturgical book) which he had brought with him to elude the charge of perjury, that is, of foreswearing upon the Gospel. The king seized his opportunity and summoned the archbishop to answer in the royal court. The biographers disagree over what followed. Some say that the archbishop fell sick and sent his excuses, which were not accepted as genuine. Others say that he produced evidence in his favour and refused to answer an unjust summons. In any case, Henry cited him once more to appear in his presence at a royal council at Northampton on 6 October.[1]

This meeting, which is covered by the biographers in very great detail, is one of the most dramatic and revealing encounters in medieval history. There are seven long narratives and several shorter accounts; two of the narratives are from eye-witnesses, William FitzStephen and Herbert of Bosham, and though they differ in details the main thread of their account is worthy of acceptance.[2] John the Marshal was missing on 6 October, but on the eighth the case was put to the council. It was similar to the case, seventy years earlier, of William of St Carilef, where a distinction was made between the bishop and the feudal vassal. The archbishop's plea was disallowed: he was pronounced guilty of feudal disobedience and contempt of the royal summons, and adjudged to have forfeited all his moveable goods to the king (£500). After the barons and the bishops had spent some time in shifting the task of

1. W. FitzStephen, *MB.*, iii. 50–1, and in detail, *EC.*, 66–7.
2. A major difference lies in the precise dating of the council and of its daily business. The text follows FitzStephen. For a full discussion see *EC.*, Appendix iv, 163–6.

pronouncing sentence from themselves, the king insisted upon common action and Henry of Winchester was told to pronounce sentence. The bishops then became guarantors for Thomas, save for Gilbert Foliot, who stood out once again from the rest.[1]

Up to this point the king had been entirely successful. Thomas had been humiliated and fined. The bishops had been caught between two loyalties and had failed both to give ready support to the king and firm adherence to Thomas. Henry would have been well advised to rest upon his success. Instead, he decided to harass his victim still further.

The next step would normally have been a re-trial of the case of John the Marshal, but here the king was on less favourable ground. The archbishop's court had probably given a just decision, and the marshal had perjured himself. The sympathy of the barons would be with the baronial court and against the new constitution. Henry, therefore, dropped the case and began a series of demands which were clearly designed to break the archbishop. The first was for money received by Thomas from the castelleries of Eye and Berkhamsted. The archbishop replied that the money had been spent on the royal service, but finally agreed on an *ex gratia* repayment, with three lay barons as his guarantors. Next day the king returned to the charge, demanding large sums for the return of an alleged loan in the Toulouse campaign and of another pledge of the king on his behalf. To this he added a demand for the presentation of accounts for all the vacant sees and abbeys of which he had had charge. Thomas replied that he had had no notice of such a demand, and that in any case he had received a formal discharge from the king shortly after his election as archbishop. Then, legally penniless and threatened with further legal processes, he demanded the time and opportunity of taking counsel.

On the next day, a Saturday, all the bishops came to Thomas's lodging in the Cluniac priory of St Andrew to take and give counsel. At first sympathy went to the archbishop, and Henry of Winchester offered to approach the king with a free-will offering of 2,000 marks.[2] His reception made it clear that the king's real object was not money but the ruin of his sometime friend and chancellor. The bishops, therefore, took it upon themselves to give their archbishop some advice. This, as might have been expected, was

1. W. FitzStephen, *MB.*, iii. 53.
2. *MB.*, iii. 54.

far from unanimous, for the occasion served as a catalyst of feeling and personal decisions influenced counsel. Gilbert Foliot, Hilary of Chichester, Robert of Lincoln and Bartholomew of Exeter were all in favour of Thomas resigning. Henry of Winchester and Roger of Worcester were alone in raising their voices for principle.[1] At last the archbishop decided to temporise and a delay was conceded. The next day was Sunday, with no official meeting, but more discussion between Thomas and the bishops. On that night the archbishop was taken ill, with an old renal complaint that may have been aggravated by the prolonged strain and anxiety.[2] He had come to the crisis of his life. To resign the archbishopric would be to admit grave error and to place himself defenceless for the king's revenge. To fight the king's monetary demands on the legal, external level would be to abandon principles for the treacherous ground of legal casuistry. Meanwhile, reports came to him of Henry's dire threats against his person. If he failed in his plea the lightest treatment would be imprisonment, which would have paralysed every activity. In this crisis, he took advice of his confessor, Robert of Merton, who counselled firmness. 'Act fearlessly,' he said, 'you have chosen God's service rather than the king's. Continue to do so, and God will not fail you.'[3] This was decisive. Early on Tuesday morning the bishops arrived at his lodging to beg him to yield to the king and resign his office; otherwise the king would have him tried for perjury and disobedience, as a disloyal subject. Thomas replied that if that should happen, the bishops must know that he had placed them under obedience to take no part in the affair. He himself appealed to Rome from the king, and ordered the bishops to excommunicate, if violence were offered, all who touched him. At this Gilbert Foliot immediately put in a counter appeal, the first of many, against Thomas's command.[4]

The archbishop then celebrated a votive Mass of St Stephen at the suggestion of Robert of Merton. It had as introit, 'Princes also

1. These details are given by Alan of Tewkesbury, *MB.*, ii. 327, who was not in England at the time. He was for some years a canon of Benevento, where Lombard, a companion of archbishop Thomas in exile, was bishop from 1171. Cf. J. C. Robertson, *MB.*, ii. p. xliii–iv.
2. For a discussion of this illness, see *EC.*, Appendix v, 167–8.
3. Anonymous I, *MB.*, iv. 45; *EC.*, 75–6.
4. H. Bosham, *MB.*, iii. 303.

lid sit and speak against me; but thy servant is occupied in thy
tatutes', and the Gospel contained a reference to Zachary slain
betwixt the temple and the altar. Then, still wearing the stole
under his cloak, and carrying the sacred Host as viaticum, he took
horse for the castle, preceded by his Welsh crossbearer, Alexander.
As he went the people crowded upon him, begging his blessing.
Dismounting in the courtyard, he took his cross from Alexander
and approached a group of bishops who were waiting, among them
Gilbert Foliot and Robert of Hereford. One of the archbishop's
clerks, Hugh of Nunant, approached Gilbert. 'My lord of London,
can you as his dean allow the archbishop to carry his own cross?'
'My dear man,' replied Gilbert, 'he has always been an ass and
always will be.'[1] Nevertheless he tried to wrench the cross from
Thomas's hands: 'If the king draws his sword and you brandish
your cross, there will be a disaster'. 'My cross is a sign of peace for
myself and the English Church', replied Thomas.

The residential part of the castle of Northampton consisted of a
large hall on the ground floor, with a smaller room on the same
level. Above was a large room, communicating with the lower
rooms by a staircase.[2] Thither the king had withdrawn when he
heard that Thomas was coming. The archbishop for his part went
into the inner room on the ground floor. At this moment Roger of
York, ostentatiously arriving late and preceded by his cross (a sign of
his equality with Thomas), passed through the hall to join the king.

Then began a long day of debate. Henry had intended to reopen
the matter of criminous clerks, but had been warned that this
would renew the solidarity between the bishops and their metropolitan. He was then told of the archbishop's appeal to Rome,
another breach of the Clarendon Constitutions. He, therefore,
returned to the matter of the ex-chancellor's accounts, to which
was added an enquiry about the appeal. Thomas answered that he
had received quittance of his debts as chancellor when he was
elected archbishop; that he had now no free cash and had exhausted
all possible guarantors. His appeal had been lodged against
suffragans who, given the occurrence, would have acted unjustly
and uncanonically.

The king then demanded that the bishops should join with the

1. W. FitzStephen, *MB.*, iii. 57. 'Bone homo, semper fuit stultus, et
semper erit'.
2. See *EC.*, Appendix vi, 169–70.

lay baronage in judging and sentencing the archbishop. The bishops were now in a fix. To obey the king would be to run counter to canonical doctrine and their own convictions, and would handicap them in any future appeal against Thomas. To refuse would be to share the fate of the archbishop. Henry urged their oath at Clarendon, but they still held out, some from fear, others from loyalty. All was now at sixes and sevens. The barons were exasperated both with the bishops and with Thomas; the bishops were bitterly divided amongst themselves and with relation to the archbishop. Throughout the day they sat in the same small room with Thomas, while messengers shuffled up and down the stairs. They were fairly caught between hammer and anvil; how could they get Thomas out of the way while remaining both pope's men and king's men? At last someone, perhaps Foliot, had an idea. They should promise the king that if he let them off pronouncing judgment on Thomas, they would appeal to the pope accusing the archbishop of forcing them to be disloyal to Henry, and would beg the pope to depose Thomas. The plan was strange enough, but it had precedents,[1] and while Thomas's enemies might hope in this way to destroy him, his friends could hope that the pope would refuse to play their game. In any case, the plan went up to the king, and he accepted it. The bishops were now committed to supporting him at the papal court; meanwhile, he could condemn the archbishop as a disloyal vassal who had revoked his promise to abide by the customary royal rights of the realm.

Henry, therefore, excused them from taking part in the trial, and they returned downstairs to sit in the lower room where Thomas sat motionless, alone save for Alexander his crossbearer and William FitzStephen and Herbert of Bosham, his future biographers. Above their heads the trial went on, and roars of 'Traitor' could be heard. The archbishop was condemned and sentenced, possibly to perpetual imprisonment, but the verdict was never declared, for when a deputation came downstairs to deliver it, the task of spokesman was passed around without any acceptance. Some had sympathy still with the archbishop; others were afraid of his curse.[2] Finally the 'good earl' of Leicester took up his

1. Anonymous I, *MB.*, iv. 49; William of Canterbury, i. 37; H. Bosham, *MB.*, iii. 308–9; *EC.*, 82–3.
2. W. FitzStephen, *MB.*, iii. 67; H. Bosham, *MB.*, iii. 349; Anonymous I, *MB.*, iv. 50–1.

parable, beginning with a long historical account of the controversy. Before he could come to the point Thomas broke in and
forbade them all to pass judgment on him. Leicester began again,
then, like Macbeth, exclaimed that he could not do it, and bade the
Earl of Cornwall continue. He too boggled, whereupon Hilary of
Chichester, whom no situation could quell, called out that the
treason was clear and bade the archbishop hear the sentence.
Thomas rose, exclaimed that they were laymen and had no right
to judge their archbishop, and strode out through the hall towards
the door. There was an uproar and shouts of 'Traitor'. Some
picked up rushes and *débris* from the floor to hurl at Thomas. In
the confusion he tripped over a cord of firewood and there was
another shout. Hamelin, the king's illegitimate half-brother and
Randolph de Broc joined in the cry of 'Traitor'. Thomas rounded
on Hamelin: 'Bastard lout! If I were not a priest, my right hand
would give you the lie. As for you (to de Broc) one of your family
has been hanged already.'[1] Then with his group of attendants he
broke out of the room. The gate of the bailey was locked, and the
porter was engaged in a private scuffle, but a bunch of keys hung
by the wall, and the first that was tried opened the door. The
archbishop's horses were at hand, and he and his followers rode off
across the town. For whatever reason, no attempt was made to
capture him. Henry may have felt that open violence would be bad
policy, as Foliot warned him.

Back at St Andrew's, Thomas sent three of his friends among
the bishops to the king, asking for permission to depart. Henry was
in good spirits, and told them he would answer next day. Thomas
supped as usual with his clerks, and gave his usual bountiful
largesse of food to the poor. Then he ordered that his bed should
be prepared in the church behind the high altar where he would
keep vigil, as he had already done on a previous night during the
council. Meanwhile an autumn gale had blown up, with a strong
wind and torrents of rain. At midnight Thomas, in disguise and
with only three companions, left the church and rode off into the
darkness and the storm. In the streets the flood water softened the
clatter of the horses' hoofs,[2] and they found one of the town gates
without a porter and unlocked. Two of his companions were lay

1. William of Canterbury, *MB.*, i. 39–40; Anonymous I, *MB.*, iv. 52.
2. Anonymous I, *MB.*, iv. 54. This writer is particularly well informed
as to the flight of the archbishop.

brothers of the Gilbertine order; the third was his own faithful personal servant. By morning he had reached Grantham, some forty miles from Northampton, whence after a short rest he rode to Lincoln, another forty miles. Here he lodged in the house of one Jacob, a fuller, the friend of one of the Gilbertine brothers. He had journeyed north to elude pursuit, which would have taken the road to London. Already, before leaving Northampton, he had given Herbert of Bosham a rendezvous at the abbey of St Bertin at St Omer, but he feared capture in England, and decided on a slow journey south. Disguising himself in the tunic and large boots of a lay brother, and taking the name of Brother Christian, he left Lincoln by boat on the Welland, and reached a hermitage (possibly the priory of Catley) belonging to the Gilbertine order, where he rested three days among the fens. Thence he passed by water to Boston, perhaps hoping for a passage to the continent, but turned back inland to the Gilbertine houses of Haverholme (Lincs.) and Chicksand (Beds.), where he picked up a canon named Gilbert and took him along. The odyssey continued with a journey to Eastry, a Canterbury manor near the coast of Thanet, where he waited for a passage.[1]

Leaving the English shore on the evening of All Souls' day (2 November), he landed in the morning darkness on the open beach of Flanders, near Gravelines. Exhausted and, so we are told, unaccustomed to walking on rough ground, he stumbled repeatedly on the shingle and finally collapsed, whereupon his companions with some difficulty procured a horse of poor quality with a straw rope for bridle. Other adventures followed, including the discovery of his identity by the wife of an innkeeper and a knight whose falcon he had examined with critical eye. Thomas was clearly quite unable to carry off a disguise; rough clothing sat upon him as unconvincingly as did a stage disguise upon Garrick. Fearing the local lords, the counts of Boulogne and Flanders, he travelled by bad roads to the Cistercian abbey of Clair-Marais, near St Omer, where he was rejoined by Herbert of Bosham, who was suitably shocked to see his master in disguise. His arrival in St Omer had coincided with that of envoys of King Henry, so the archbishop again took to the marshes for a few days before going to the abbey of St Bertin, where he was honourably received.[2]

1. Anonymous I, *MB.*, iv. 55 and H. Bosham, *MB.*, iii. 323-4.
2. Anonymous I, *MB.*, iv. 56-8 is very full here.

CHAPTER 7

Exile, 1164-66

WITH THE landing of archbishop Thomas on foreign soil at the beginning of November 1164, there began a period of six years, which was full of fruitless discussion and perpetual frustration for all concerned, and of which much of the tedium can be felt by all who try to follow the course of events in various circles as given by half-a-dozen incomplete and often contradictory narratives. Moreover, during this period the affairs of the archbishop of Canterbury became entangled in the web of European history, which must, therefore, be considered in its broad contemporary outlines. Four continental powers, at odds among themselves, influenced the course of events. The king of England, who was also the ruler, on various titles, of the western half of what is modern France; the king of France, threatened on almost every side by his powerful neighbours; the Emperor Frederick I, a perpetual threat to Italy and a potential threat to France; and the Pope, Alexander III. The last-named, as the most directly affected of the continental potentates, may be mentioned first.

The English Pope Hadrian IV had died in 1159 after a reign of five years and at a moment of crisis in his relations with the emperor. His right-hand man in the implementation of his policy had been the Sienese cardinal Roland Bandinelli, a celebrated professor of Bologna and later cardinal and papal chancellor. At the election which took place almost immediately, cardinal Roland obtained a clear majority of votes, but canon law had as yet made no provision for a contested election, and the minority of the cardinals who were of the imperial party were the first to robe and crown their candidate, while his rival, who took the name of

Alexander III, was besieged for a week in the Castel Sant'Angelo, and then fled from Rome.[1]

Rallying his supporters he acted with determination, and carried on the papal government with the distinction of a great lawyer and able theologian. The reputation of Alexander III has suffered at the hands of some English historians by reason of his apparently hesitant and ambiguous attitude in the years of Thomas's exile. It may be granted that he was not cast in the mould of Gregory VII or Innocent III, but it must not be forgotten that, like other popes in times of crisis in other centuries, as head of the Church he had to consider not only his own uncertain situation, but the interests of the Church as a whole among the warring factions of Europe. Whether he sometimes judged ill, or whether he was in fact a better judge of his age than a modern historian can be, are matters of opinion, but it is certain that the better the years of his pontificate are becoming known, the higher does his reputation stand.[2] He is the first of a line of great administrators and lawyers who occupied the papal throne for more than a century with some intervals. Though neither a saint nor a personality of the first order, he was perhaps the greatest pope of the twelfth century before Innocent III. Certainly he was the one who set his stamp most firmly on the doctrinal and moral teaching of the Church, and still more upon its body of administrative law. He clarified the canonical status of exemption from episcopal jurisdiction for monastic bodies, he established the process of canonisation, and he defined the essentials of a valid marriage.

Seeking refuge in France from the attacks of Frederick I and the intrigues of the Romans, he remained north of the Alps for almost four years, from March 1162 to November 1165. During all this time he was warding off the German emperor and his antipope by firmness and diplomacy, while at the same time endeavouring to make sure of the support of both Louis VII of France and the more powerful and far more slippery king of England, who was ruler of a

1. The celebrated decree of 1059 assumed a final agreement among the cardinals. Alexander himself, at the Third Lateran Council of 1179, fixed the necessary majority at two-thirds for an election. For the English view of Alexander's election, see *JS.*, *Ep.* 124 and notes, and *GFL.*, no. 133 and notes (especially p. 176 n. 4).
2. For Alexander see M. Pacaut, *Alexandre III*, Paris 1956, and M. W. Baldwin, *Alexander III and the Twelfth Century*, New York 1968.

continental complex of territories from the Pyrenees to the straits of Dover. The episode of Thomas of Canterbury was, from the point of view of papal diplomacy, a vexatious and gratuitous nuisance, and its settlement by compromise would have been of the greatest political advantage. That Alexander, dealing with two powerful, obstinate and potentially unstable men engaged in mortal combat, should have maintained his prestige and kept the initiative with a minimum of double-dealing, is evidence enough of his skill and firmness.

Louis VII, a long-lived king who reigned from 1137 to 1180, was for his contemporaries a smaller and less brilliant, though possibly more admirable, man than his two fellow-monarchs, Henry and Frederick. Nevertheless, his reign in the long run was as significant for his country as were theirs. Left free to go crusading in his youth by the administrative and personal reliability of the great abbot Suger, and married to the most remarkable woman of the age, Eleanor of Aquitaine, he had committed a political blunder of the first magnitude by obtaining a separation from her, thus leaving her free to give herself and Aquitaine to the young Henry of Anjou. Thenceforward Henry by turns fought, outwitted, despoiled and made friends with her sometime-husband in one of the most remarkable political love-hate relationships of medieval Europe. From all this, Louis VII emerged as a basically loyal and devout man, generous in his aid to the exiled pope and the exiled archbishop. Indeed, had he failed these two, it is hard to see how their fortunes could have survived. Yet Louis, though genuinely devout and moderate, slowly and noiselessly strengthened the position of the crown as against the Church by controlling elections and claiming regalian rights. Though less violent and provocative than Henry or Frederick, he nevertheless met with considerable success in his control of the Church and of his kingdom.

The third power was that of Frederick Barbarossa, who ruled from 1152 to 1190. In church polity his aim throughout his reign was to restore the royal and imperial control to what it had been in pre-Gregorian days. The schism of 1159 was an uncovenanted mercy to him, and so long as it lasted he was able, with the help of subservient anti-popes, to achieve his purpose with some success. He could speak of Rome as his fief and of the pope as his vassal, Yet, in Germany, where traditions of St Boniface still survived, there were always individual bishops who stood out for Gregorian principles and took the side of Alexander III. By and large, however, his firm control of the Church, especially in the years when his chancellor Rainald of Dassel was in power, remained a standing pattern for Henry II of England to observe. Henry must have been familiar with German conditions from his mother, and it must have seemed to the pope that Henry was far more likely to break with him and join the emperor than was Louis VII.

Arrived in France, Alexander III, having countered an attempt of Frederick to capture his person with the assistance (which was not forthcoming) of Louis, met the kings of France and England near Tours in September 1162. Here, the two kings were reconciled from their latest quarrel, and paid honour to the pope in company. Nine months later Alexander held a council at Tours, at which the archbishop of Canterbury arrived in considerable state, and where he sat on the right hand of the pope. Thus from this occasion onwards Alexander had personal knowledge of both the king of England and his archbishop. As we have seen, he endeavoured to bring about a *détente* in the growing hostility between Henry and Thomas, and was doubtless disappointed by the affair of Clarendon. Whatever his desire for accommodation and peace, he could not approve of all the Constitutions, though he probably thought that they were not intended to be taken very seriously.

After Thomas had left Northampton, King Henry had taken counsel as to his next step. Advised by Foliot and others, he selected an embassy to approach the pope and urge the deposition of the archbishop. They were a powerful group. Their leader, Gilbert Foliot, bishop of London, was accompanied by Roger of York, Hilary of Chichester, Bartholomew of Exeter and Roger of Worcester, and also by a group of barons including the earl of Arundel, several barons of the exchequer, and two clerks, John of Oxford and Richard of Ilchester, who were to remain in the fore-front of the king's party and ultimately to receive bishoprics. Their instructions were to establish the just dealing and moderation of the king, and to persuade the pope to give summary judgment on archbishop Thomas. Failing that, they were to ask for a legate to try the case in Thomas's presence in England.[1]

As we have seen, they arrived at St Omer simultaneously with the archbishop. Meanwhile, Herbert of Bosham had reached the

1. H. Bosham, *MB.*, iii. 336–7; FitzStephen, iii. 74.

papal court to give an eyewitness's account of the Council of Northampton; he had previously waited on King Louis and obtained his promise of help.

While Herbert was pressing his cause upon the pope, archbishop Thomas was seeing better days. After resting at St Omer he was escorted to Soissons by Milo, bishop of Thérouanne and the abbot of St Bertin. King Louis arrived at Soissons the next day, and promised his financial aid to the exile so long as he might need it. From the king Thomas proceeded to Alexander III at Sens.

Meanwhile the embassy from England had arrived at the papal court. Gilbert Foliot opened the proceedings by an account of the Council of Northampton, that developed into a recrimination of the archbishop which was cut short by Alexander with a reproof: 'Gently, brother, gently'. 'Holy father, I will spare him', replied Gilbert. 'It was not for him but for yourself that I felt anxious', said the pope.[1] Gilbert was disconcerted, and gave way to Hilary of Chichester who, as an old advocate in the Curia, prided himself on his knowledge of the wicket, though his foibles also were doubtless well known to many of his hearers. He roundly attacked the archbishop: '*Et certe virum tantae auctoritatis id non decuit, nec oportuit, nec aliquando oportuebat, . . . insuper suos si saperent non oportuerit. . . .*' At this point his attempts to conjugate and deploy an impersonal verb were drowned in the laughter of the assembled fathers, and some shouted; 'Try another port'.[2] Hilary retired, and it was left for the moderate Bartholomew to ask for legates, and for the tactful earl of Arundel, speaking in French, to ask the pope to intervene in the matter. Alexander was hard pressed, and a legate who should decide without leave for an appeal was demanded, but the pope stood firm: 'I will not give my glory to another'.[3] The envoys, who had been strictly enjoined not to remain in the Curia, returned to England and reported to the king. When they had departed, the archbishop was graciously received. He read the Constitutions of Clarendon in full to the consistory, and the pope condemned them a second time. According to a trustworthy

1. Alan of Tewkesbury, *MB.*, ii. 338. Gilbert had quoted *Proverbs* xxviii, 1, 'The wicked flee when no man pursueth'.
2. 'Male tandem venisti ad portum'. Alan of Tewkesbury, *MB.*, ii. 338–9. His account is borne out by an almost contemporary letter of Herbert of Bosham, *MB.*, v. (177), 341–2.
3. Alan of Tewkesbury, *MB.*, ii. 341.

biographer, he then confessed his weakness in yielding to the king, and begged to be allowed to resign his see, but the pope, freeing him from his oath at Clarendon, confirmed him as archbishop and recognised the primacy of Canterbury.[1]

It was now clear to all that no speedy end to the controversy could be expected, and the archbishop and his companions decided to take up residence at a religious house away from the disturbed atmosphere of the papal court. They chose Pontigny, a celebrated Cistercian abbey at no great distance from Sens, one of the four 'first daughters' of Cîteaux. The pope accordingly wrote a letter of recommendation and the move was made. Pontigny was a prosperous house, and could absorb the group without suffering a shortage for the community. Thomas, heir to the tradition that archbishops of Canterbury should be, or should become, monks, begged of the pope a monastic habit. Alexander blessed and sent him one of rough cloth, with the message: 'Tell him we have sent the only one we have'.[2]

The archbishop's exile lasted for almost exactly six years, from 2 November 1164 to 2 December 1170. Most recent accounts of his life treat this period summarily, and not without excuse. While the main story is simple and the climax unusually well documented, it is not easy to construct a detailed year-by-year narrative. None of the biographers is both full and wholly accurate, and alongside of their narratives runs a long series of some seven hundred letters, some of them in narrative form, very few of them dated, and all written by interested parties in the heat of conflict. Though the original collection and the printed editions based upon it maintain a fair chronological order, there are numerous undatable items, and a few that are clearly out of order in the collection of the Rolls Series. The difficulties of the critic and the ennui of the reader are increased by the frequent repetition in different letters of similar narratives and similar arguments, while many of the letters consist of a stream of words carrying a minimum of factual information. Nevertheless, their careful perusal is necessary, for unless one has read through the whole *corpus* one cannot appreciate the strains and stresses to which individuals of every party were subjected, nor can one form a solid judgment on the characters and insights

1. W. FitzStephen, *MB.*, iii. 76; cf. H. Bosham, *MB.*, iii. 340 ff.
2. Alan of Tewkesbury, *MB.*, ii. 345. 'Misimus qualem habuimus, non qualem vellemus.'

of the various leading actors. Above all, a careful study is essential for anyone who would assess the mental and spiritual qualities of the protagonist, archbishop Thomas. Historians and readers can easily tire and become censorious of the leaders in a prolonged controversy in which neither side gives any tangible sign of a desire for any kind of accommodation. A moment's thought, however, will provide us with many instances from the political and diplomatic scene of our own day of controversies that were equally prolonged, sterile and apparently both needless and useless. And, when the central figure is a man of stature in his own right as well as being the head of the Church in England, we are under obligation to examine his cause very closely before passing judgment upon him.

During these six years we have to reckon with the designs, actions and interactions of three main centres of activity: the exiled archbishop, the king of England, and the pope. Each of these was surrounded by a group of close adherents; the archbishop by his household of clerks and agents, the king by his counsellors, ministers and royal clerks, the pope by his cardinals and curial assistants. Each party, moreover, could count on supporters outside the main field of action, and correspondents of varying degrees of trustworthiness. The archbishop, during the whole period, was domiciled first at Pontigny and then near Sens, with occasional excursions to conferences. The king continued his life of movement in his English and continental dominions. He was in England from January 1163 to March 1166 save for two months (March–May 1165) abroad. He was in Normandy and elsewhere on the continent from March 1166 till March 1170, then in England from March to June, when he went abroad again. The pope was at Sens from September 1163 till April 1165, after which he went to Italy and was in Rome and its neighbourhood. The historian has, therefore, the awkward task of remembering when and where these three groups of action were in contact, or at least within easy reach of one another by letter, and when they were separated by the English Channel or by several hundred miles of road. There were, in addition, two other groups: the French king, with his brother Henry, archbishop of Rheims, and his courtiers, and the English bishops, never after Northampton a united body either physically or morally, but retaining some real influence and considerable potential power. Beside these groups there were a few influential men outside the circle of satellites. Of these the most important was John of Salisbury, in exile since the autumn of 1163 and living his own life, for most of the time with Peter of Celle, now abbot of S. Rémi at Rheims. Others were John of Canterbury, Thomas's ally of other days, now bishop of Poitiers, and William, archbishop of Sens, both friendly to the archbishop; and on the other side Arnulf of Lisieux and Rotrou, archbishop of Rouen.

Having settled at Pontigny, the archbishop increased the austerity of his life. He had worn a hairshirt habitually since becoming archbishop, and had received the discipline frequently. Now he lived sparingly and shared the coarse diet of the monks. He fell ill, and Herbert remonstrated with him to good effect.[1] Throughout his stay at Pontigny he atoned (as he said) for past neglect by a study of theology, that is, in the context of the time, principally the study of Scripture; and here he had in Herbert of Bosham one of the most distinguished scripture scholars of his day, despite his tedious verbosity as a biographer.[2] The Psalms, we are told, and the Epistles were his main subjects of meditation and study, but Herbert tells us also that he and the archbishop sat at the feet of Lombard of Piacenza, later archbishop of Benevento, who taught them canon law. A report of this activity must have reached John of Salisbury, who took it upon himself to read the archbishop an epistolary lesson on the superiority of the Psalms and the *Morals* of Gregory the Great over legal studies. 'Whoever,' asked John, 'rose from a study of the civil or even of the canon law with a humbled and a contrite heart?'[3]

By this time also a certain number of Thomas's household had rejoined him. Herbert notes, besides Lombard of Piacenza, Reginald the Lombard (who defaulted later), Gerard la Pucelle and Hugh of Nunant (defaulters also), Gilbert Glanville, Gunter of Winchester, Roland and Arnald of Lombardy, Humbert of Bourges, and Alexander Llewellyn, who alone stands out as a

---

1. *MB.*, iii. 377–8.
2. There is an account of Bosham's scholarship, which included a knowledge of Hebrew, in B. Smalley, *The Study of the Bible in the Middle Ages*, 2 ed., Oxford 1952, and a fuller one in her forthcoming work *The Becket Conflict and the Schools*.
3. *MB.*, v. (85), 163. 'Quis a lectione legum, aut etiam canonum, compunctus surgit?'

recognisable personality. 'He was,' says Herbert, 'Welsh in name and by birth, a man of education and of a pleasant wit. He was not only strong in words, but in deeds also. He was a help to our father sometimes of his own accord, sometimes under obedience and sometimes on a mission. He was often in danger, but acted with care, with firmness and with constancy. Finally, what is a great thing in a Welshman, he was not only efficient, but faithful to his master always and everywhere'.[1] He had, indeed, licence both to rebuke and to chaff the archbishop, with something of the function of the Fool in *King Lear*, though Llewellyn was no fool.

Besides his returning clerks, Thomas had other visitors at Pontigny. The embassy sent to the pope had returned to the king with the story of their failure. Henry, who was not usually pitiless, proceeded to send into exile all Thomas's kin, young and old, men and women, with instructions that they were to seek out the archbishop and show him their plight. Herbert of Bosham describes the exiles as coming in droves to Pontigny, men, women and children in arms.[2] No doubt he exaggerates, but the hardship was genuine, though the exiles found both sympathy and charity in France. The next to suffer were the clerks of the archbishop, who were dispossessed of their benefices and prebends while their mothers and fathers, sisters and brothers, nephews and nieces (so Henry's writ to his sheriffs specified) were to have their persons and goods put to bail at the king's pleasure.[3] Finally, the archbishop's Canterbury estates were handed over to his old enemies, the Broc family, to farm.[4]

At about the same time the archbishop attempted to secure a mediator in the person of the empress, Henry's mother. He wrote deploring the king's conduct and asking her to remonstrate. A little later he sent a friend to urge her in person. The latter reported that the lady was of tyrants' brood herself and in favour of some of the Constitutions of Clarendon. She had, indeed, acted herself on occasion in a thoroughly pre-Gregorian fashion with bishops'

1. *MB.*, iii. 528. 'Quod in natione illa valde pretiosum, sicut operans, ita . . . fidem servans'.
2. *MB.*, iii. 359. 'Parvuli etiam in cunabulis et ad matrum adhuc pendentes ubera'. This massive banishment shocked contemporary sentiment and must influence any estimate of Henry's humanity.
3. *MB.*, v. (78), 152.
4. *Ibid.*

elections, and she now provided a very comprehensive list of the delinquences of criminous clerks—a list that has been repeated without acknowledgment by modern historians. Nevertheless, she could give very good advice. The Constitutions, she said, should never have been written down, and her recipe for peace was that the written document and the oaths of the bishops should alike be cancelled. After that, royal justices should be told to be careful, and bishops to be reasonable.[1]

Meanwhile, early in 1165, Alexander III explored various avenues. He wrote to Gilbert Foliot, asking him to mollify the king, and in June he wrote again, bidding Gilbert to take Robert of Hereford with him and to take Henry to task for his treatment of Thomas; the pope added to Gilbert a commission to collect the outstanding Peter's Pence. Foliot duly replied that he had caught up with the king at Shrewsbury, and had found him amenable to criticism, and willing to receive the archbishop back if the royal rights were respected. The bishop urged the pope to treat the king gently.[2] While this was going on, the pope's peace of mind was disturbed by a move from Barbarossa. In the spring of 1165 Rainald of Dassel, as imperial chancellor, met Henry II at Rouen to fix up a marriage agreement between the king's daughter Matilda and Henry the Lion, Duke of Saxony. He used the occasion to exploit the coolness between Henry and Alexander III in the emperor's favour, and was so far successful as to carry back to Germany John of Oxford and Richard of Ilchester, two of Henry's ablest confidential clerks.[3] Whether by accident or design he arrived at Würzburg on Whit Monday, in the middle of an imperial court summoned to discuss ways and means of coming to terms with Alexander. Rainald successfully stampeded Frederick and the diet into decreeing an oath of perpetual hostility to Alexander and support of the antipope Paschal. The two Englishmen, observed by Gerard la Pucelle, who had left the service of the archbishop and was in Cologne at the time, took the oath, with momentous consequences. Soon after their return to England, Henry, by way of rewarding John of Oxford, recommended him to Jocelin of Salisbury for the vacant deanery of his cathedral. This was

1. Nicolas of Mont St Jacques to Thomas, *MB.*, v. (76), 148–51. 'Mulier de genere tyrannorum est'.
2. *MB.*, v. (108), 207; *GFL.*, no. 155.
3. *MB.*, v. (97), 182 ff., especially 193.

doubly illegal, both because John was in schism on account of his oath against Alexander III at Würzburg, and because some of the canonical electors to the deanery were in exile with the archbishop, who had obtained from the pope a specific prohibition against any election while they were absent.[1] The appointment was, therefore, quashed by the pope, and Jocelin, who had permitted it to be made, fell irremediably into the black books of the archbishop.

Between May 1165, and the end of the year it seems impossible to follow any moves in the controversy. The letters that can be dated with certainty to this interval are chiefly those from the archbishop to settle administrative details in England and Wales, and from the pope soliciting English help for Thomas. In the autumn of 1165 Alexander left France and reached Rome and Italy. Henceforward we have always to remember that he was at least a month behind any event in northern France or England, and that his pondered reaction would be another six or seven weeks in coming. This was the best that could be hoped for, but, in fact, the pope was perpetually harried by the emperor's hostility and warfare in Italy, and we can only admire his perseverance in attention to the case which must have seemed to him an unfortunate and undesirable hindrance to his policy in western Europe.

Early in 1166 Thomas attempted to bring Henry to a better frame of mind by three personal letters. They are the only letters of his in which the controversial and the pastoral notes are heard together. Thomas was not a great letter-writer, and even here the sense of personal emotion and persuasive urgency is almost entirely lacking. We cannot but think of the dazzling display of fireworks and deep spiritual wisdom with which Bernard would have improved the occasion. The archbishop is stilted and heavy, and we cannot help remembering, as perhaps he did also, the Becket who jousted and roistered with his young king a dozen years earlier. The first letter, beginning with the words *Loqui de Deo*, is sober in tone. 'To speak of God demands a mind wholly calm and free. It is so with me because I am about to speak to my lord—would that he were a prince of peace to all'. Henry is 'my most beloved lord, my most serene prince'. The archbishop begs for relief for the sorely tried Church in England, and warns

1. *MB.*, v. (199), 398.

him of the consequence of a refusal.[1] The second is longer and
more severe. '*Expectans expectavi*—Long have I waited for the
Lord to look upon you that you might do penance and leave
the evil way', and the writer goes on to give a statement of the
paramount authority of the spiritual power, taken from the
familiar letter of Gelasius I and the letter of Gregory VII to
Herman of Metz. The tone is still moderate, but the superiority
of the priesthood to the royal power is stressed, and Henry is
exhorted to remember the brevity and the vanity of human
and of kingly life.[2] The third begins with the words of Christ,
'Long have I desired—*Diu desideravi*—to see your face and
to speak with you', and asserts once more the paramount jurisdiction of the spiritual power. Let Henry remember the oath
that he took at his coronation at Westminster. If he will ensure
the liberty of the Church, and restore to the see of Canterbury
all that he has taken away, the archbishop will gladly return and
obey him in all things lawful to a bishop.[3] The two first letters
were presented by Urban, a Cistercian, who reported failure to
influence the king. The third was delivered by an ascetic, brother
Gerard, who bore also a personal message from the archbishop.
Gerard was noted for his blunt and direct speech, and he gave of
his best to the king. But on this occasion, at least, Henry gave
him a draught of his own medicine, and he returned with a
dusty answer to the archbishop.[4] Thomas, somewhat unexpectedly,
was disappointed that the letters had had no effect, and seriously
considered once more the advisability of resigning his office, but
he was deterred by the unanimous disapproval of his companions,
and decided on more active measures.

The pope had hitherto kept to his policy of temporising. He
had every reason to avoid antagonising Henry, and the king
had his agents at the Curia. Moreover, Alexander was by tempera-

1. *MB.*, v. (152), 266–8.
2. *MB.*, v. (153), 269–78. There is uncertainty as to which of the two
letters *Expectans* and *Diu desideravi* came first. I have followed Robertson
and others, though without firm conviction.
3. *MB.*, v. (154), 278–82.
4. H. Bosham, *MB.*, iii. 385. 'Quin potius dura propinantes, dura pro
duris, immo multo plus duriora prioribus, reportarunt.' Could this have
been the Brother Gerard, later at Witham, who gave Henry another dose
ten years later? Cf. Knowles, *The Monastic Order in England*, 2 ed.,
Cambridge 1963, 383.

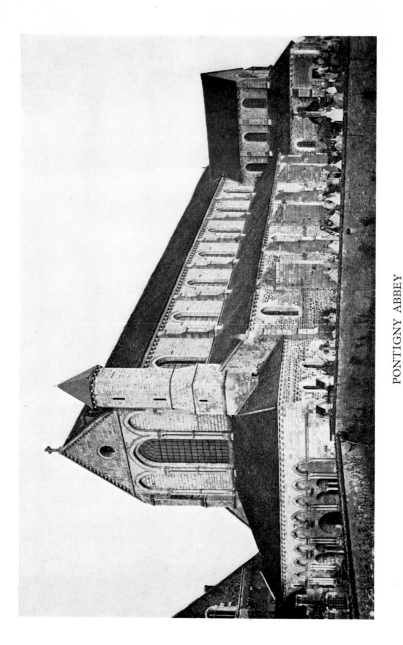

PONTIGNY ABBEY

Pontigny was founded in 1114, one of the 'four elder daughters' of Cîteaux.
The church, dating from 1140–50, is a fine example of the second generation

nent unsympathetic to the fire and bravura of Thomas. The
latter now desired to strike hard at his opponents, convinced,
and probably with justice, that nothing but threats of excommunication would bring Henry to a change of mind. Now, in the
spring of 1166, the pope relaxed the prohibition he had made
in the preceding June, and on Easter Day, 24 April, he announced
that Thomas had been appointed papal legate in the province of
Canterbury. He had recently allowed the archbishop to proceed
against those who had invaded Canterbury property.[1] Henry for
his part, fearing excommunication, called an assembly of bishops
at Chinon, who, at the suggestion of Arnulf of Lisieux, decided
to appeal against any future action of Thomas. The latter, meanwhile, after a pilgrimage to Soissons, proceeded to Vézelay for
Whitsuntide, with the intention of excommunicating Henry on
Whit Sunday.[2] On the Friday before the feast, however, he
received news of the king's serious illness. He therefore changed
his purpose and, preaching at Mass on the Sunday in the basilica,
which was crowded with pilgrims and others, he began by reciting
the history of Clarendon and the king's subsequent violence and
injustice. Then after threatening extreme measures unless
Henry repented, he proceeded to suspend Jocelin of Salisbury
for admitting John of Oxford to his deanery, and continued by
excommunicating John himself, Richard of Ilchester, his companion at Würzburg, Richard de Luci, Jocelin de Balliol, Randulph
de Broc and other lesser barons, who were in possession of
Canterbury estates.[3] This produced a sheaf of appeals. One was
in the name of the bishops of England. The archbishop followed
this up by a letter to all the bishops of his province, demanding
their help in implementing the censures, and ordering the bishop
of London to circulate his letter. The bishops replied by a letter
to the pope, composed by Foliot. The king, they say, is the most
Christian of monarchs, the most faithful of husbands, who desires
nothing but the elimination of all sin from his realm. Unfortunately a pious dispute (*sancta quaedam contentio*) has arisen over

1. *MB.*, v. (164), 316.
2. H. Bosham, *MB.*, iii. 391. The excommunication was a surprise
even to his companions—'nec enim . . . nobis hoc indicavit.' Herbert
strangely mistakes the date, which was Whit Sunday, and not as he
gives it, the patronal feast of St Mary Magdalene, 22 July. Cf. John of
Salisbury, *MB.*, v. (194), 382–3.
3. *MB.*, v. (195), 388.

criminous clerks in which both parties have the purest of intentions
As for the king, he merely put forward some traditional custom
which he would willingly have modified. All has been ruined
by the outrageous conduct of the archbishop, who has now added
to his previous threats by hurling excommunications around
They, therefore, appeal against him fixing the term for Ascension
Day, 1167[1]. The bishops wrote also to Thomas, Foliot once more
taking the pen, praising the king and warning the archbishop
of the dangers of his violence.[2] Nevertheless, Foliot was in a
quandary. His training as a monk and a Gregorian had given him
a reverence for ecclesiastical obedience that nothing could
eradicate, and he could not bring himself to deny Thomas's
jurisdiction both as archbishop and legate. He therefore wrote
to the king, begging him to permit the bishops to obey Thomas
in collecting Peter's Pence, and to restore their benefices to the
exiled clerks, while at the same time appealing to the pope against
his impossible behaviour.[3] John of Salisbury, hearing of the appeal
wrote to Thomas suggesting that he should call out to himself
some of the bishops for discussion. He followed this up with
another letter, in which he recommended moderation, and
discouraged action against the king, but urged Thomas to stand
by his principles without fear of the martyrdom that might
come.[4]

Meanwhile, the bishops (or rather Foliot) wrote to the archbishop praising the king as one who loves to be reprimanded if
he has acted wrongly. Thomas passed on this and other letters
to John of Salisbury who, after a careful study, gave his confident
opinion that they were the work of Achitophel assisted by Doeg—
Gilbert Foliot and Robert of Hereford—and that the other
bishops merely followed his lead.[5] A letter written almost at
the same time to Bartholomew of Exeter is even more scathing

1. *MB.*, v. (204), 403–8; *GFL.*, no. 166.
2. *MB.*, v. (205), 408–13; *GFL.*, no. 167.
3. *MB.*, v. (208), 417–8; *GFL.*, no. 168, July 1166.
4. *MB.*, v. (215), 435–7; (217) 439–42. Did Thomas remember this
when John told him on his last day that nobody but himself (Thomas)
desired martyrdom? See below p. 144. It is possible that the order of
these two letters should be reversed.
5. *MB.*, vi. (231), 15. 'Nonne stylus ipse convincit Achitophel et Doech?'
The letters around the division between vols. v. and vi. of *MB.*, have
got badly out of order. Cf. *GF.*, pp. 31, 166.

How can they have the nerve, the impudence, the face, to write of Henry's piety, gentleness, justice and affability when his outrageous conduct is common talk and all the world knows his trickery and violence. "We do not say that the lord king never sinned, but we say and proclaim with confidence that he is always ready to make satisfaction to the Lord." If they want people to believe them, let them get beyond the bounds of Europe, else all who hear will bellow at them: "Tell that to the marines" '.[1] John and the exiles had been disturbed to hear that Robert of Hereford, well known in the schools of Paris as Robert of Melun, was regarded as an ally of Gilbert and a prime mover against the archbishop. 'What shall I say of Hereford? Only that in the past, before he appeared in his true colours, he stood out as the shadow of a name, if not of a great one. He is now willing to act as Bibulus to Caesar Gilbert'. He advised Thomas to get someone such as the prior of St Victor to write to him.[2] The prior duly obliged, and having had the advantage of reading John's earlier letter, was able to make use of some of its telling phrases, including the effective tag from Horace.[3] Finally, Thomas wrote to all the bishops (this was a long, turgid and rambling missive in Herbert of Bosham's best style and may have been merely a draft never sent), to the clergy (a long *apologia pro vita sua*), and finally, a shorter and more pungent letter, not wholly in the best taste, to Gilbert himself.[4] This called forth all Gilbert's powers, and he replied with the celebrated letter *Multiplicem*. 'Your letter, reverend father, contains such a flood of charges of all kinds . . .'. In it he traverses the whole story once more, greatly to the disadvantage of the archbishop, in what is in effect a long speech for the prosecution, in which Henry is presented as a model husband tearing himself from the

1. *MB.*, vi. (252), 69. 'Quaere peregrinum, vicinia rauca reclament'. Cf. Horace, *Epistles* I. xvii, last line. Literally: 'all the neighbourhood will roar, "Find a stranger to tell that one to" '. The line is cited in a similar context by the abbot and prior of St Victor (*MB.*, v. (220), 458) and there are other similarities between their letter and that of John, which the authors must surely have seen. The order of the letters is faulty.

2. *MB.*, vi. (231), 16, 20. Note also quotations from Suetonius and Juvenal.

3. *MB.*, v. (220), 458. The letters have been misplaced; cf. p. 114 nn. 4–5 above.

4. *MB.*, v. (221), 459 ff.; (223) 490 ff.; (224) 512 ff. Cf. *GFL.*, p. 219.

society of a chaste wife and darling children to follow the Lord
Jesus carrying his cross in naked poverty [Gilbert had forgotten
his account earlier in the letter of Henry's tyrannous use of
force to secure Becket's election] while Thomas leaves his
colleagues [to the tender mercies of the model king] and cries
to heaven—for the income he has left behind. 'Even the Jews,
my father, were sickened by the sight of the price of blood'.
This exchange of letters, as might have been expected, closed
the correspondence.

1. *MB.*, v. (225), 538; *GFL.*, p. 240. 'Et annui vestri redditus, nunquid
vobis tanti sunt ut fratrum vestrorum sanguine vobis hos velitis acquiri?
At Juda reportante pecuniam hanc Judei respuerunt, quoniam sanguinis
esse pretium agnoverunt.' Cf. *GF.*, 172.

CHAPTER 8

Exile, 1166-70

HENRY met the excommunications by an embassy to the pope, which he sent by way of imperial territory to give an impression of solidarity between himself and Frederick. In his letter announcing this to Rainald of Dassel, now archbishop of Cologne, he gives as members of his party the archbishop of York, the bishop of London, John of Oxford and Richard de Luci.[1] Thomas sent emissaries to oppose the king's party. Meanwhile, the king wrote to the general chapter of the Cistercians, due to meet on 14 September, threatening confiscation of their English possessions if they continued to harbour his enemy. When news of this came to Pontigny, the archbishop, to save his hosts from harm or embarrassment announced his departure and left in November amid general lamentation.[2] King Louis, hearing this, offered the exiles hospitality in any abbey of France; they chose St Colomba at Sens, and remained there for four years, while the archbishop continued his regime of penance. This gave Herbert of Bosham, writing many years later, the opportunity to break out into praise of France and its people; 'Sweet France, truly sweet is she . . . her people have made drunken with delight all those that came to her, with the cup of her sweetness.'[3] There can, indeed, be few examples of such hospitality and forbearance as King Louis and many individuals among his subjects showed to an exiled archbishop and his many dependents and relatives for so long a space of time.

Alexander accepted the appeal of the bishops on 1 December 1166 and declared his intention of sending legates to England. Meanwhile, he had restrained Thomas from hurling any more

1. *MB.*, v. (213), 428.
2. H. Bosham, *MB.*, iii. 397–404.
3. *MB.*, iii. 407–8.

anathemas, and allowed that any of those already excommunicated might be absolved by any of the bishops if he were in danger of death. Thomas, as might be expected, took this ill. It was the result, as he knew, of John of Oxford's successful diplomacy at Rome, though he had had to join in condemning some of the constitutions of Clarendon in order to win these concessions from Alexander. Envoys were duly despatched on 1 January 1167, namely, cardinals William and Otto, who, in Roman diplomatic fashion, represented the two interests concerned, William being the king's friend.

Meanwhile, Thomas had taken the advice of John of Salisbury and had called out some of the bishops to Sens to meet him for an interview. This had hit the bishop of London hard, but in spite of prohibitory letters from Henry, who was abroad at the time, he had begun his journey and was whistling for a wind at Southampton when John of Oxford came ashore on his way back from Rome, with the welcome news that the pope as well as the king forbade his crossing.[1] 'Thomas will never again be my archbishop' was Foliot's joyful response. The pope's action, however, did not go unchallenged. It drew from John of Salisbury an indignant and outspoken letter. Why has the pope acted thus? Henry was on the point of yielding when the news came that he was off the hook. The pope has indeed plenary power, but not to change the laws of God and of nature. He has given *carte blanche* to Henry against all justice and sound policy. 'I may be speaking strongly', adds John, 'but my mind is burning with anguish and I cannot control it.'[2] John's anger is all the more impressive in view of the plea he had repeatedly put in to Thomas to spare Jocelin of Salisbury and his son—a plea that had gone also to the pope. At the same time, John, with his characteristic moderation, is found restraining Thomas from abusing William of Pavia, the unacceptable legate. His letter of reproach to Alexander had its effect, and in May the cardinal legates received instructions not to enter England till peace has been made between Thomas and the king,[3] and nothing is heard of their movements till November, when a meeting with the archbishop and the

1. Letter of Thomas to his envoy at the papal court, *MB.*, vi. (285), 150–2; cf. *ibid.*, (292) 172–3.
2. *MB.*, vi. (295), 176–9.
3. *MB.*, vi. (307), 200–2 (May 1166); cf. no. 324 of August.

king was fixed for a place between Gisors and Trie on 18 November.

This was the first of a long series of attempts to persuade the king and Thomas to come to an understanding. The legates first interviewed the archbishop, begging him to yield to the king's demands or alternatively to submit to their verdict in arbitration. The archbishop, who was accompanied by John of Salisbury, Herbert of Bosham, Lombard of Piacenza and others, read out once more the Constitutions of Clarendon and refused to retreat from his condition that he would only promise observance with the proviso 'saving the honour of God, the liberty of the Church, fair treatment for himself and restitution of the confiscated lands of Canterbury'. The Constitutions were unprecedented, and had been condemned by the pope. Would he, it was asked, let them pass without a word for or against? It is an English proverb, he replied, that silence implies consent.[1] The cardinals, disappointed in their meeting with Thomas, went on to meet the king and some of the bishops near Argentan on 27 November. This meeting also was unproductive, and the king exclaimed angrily that he hoped he would never set eyes on another cardinal.[2] The bishops, on their side, heard Gilbert Foliot rehearse the archbishop's misdeeds before he, together with Jocelin of Salisbury and Henry of Winchester, appealed once more to the pope. At the end of it all, the king begged the cardinals to ask the pope to free him altogether from Thomas, and wept before them all. Cardinal William mingled his tears with those of the king, while Cardinal Otto suppressed a guffaw.[3]

There followed an undignified tussle of jurisdiction, some of those excommunicated by the archbishop asserting that the danger of crossing the Channel or going to Wales satisfied the condition imposed by the pope for their absolution, while Thomas

1. *MB.*, vi. (332, 334), 257–8, 264–5.
2. *MB.*, vi. (339), 270. 'Utinam nunquam amplius videat oculus meus aliquem cardinalem.' We are reminded of the Duke of Suffolk's outburst when Cardinal Campeggio adjourned the divorce court of Catherine of Aragon: 'By the Mass, now I see that the old said saw is true, that there was never legate nor cardinal, that did good in England.' (*Hall's Chronicle*, ed. C. Whibley, London 1904, ii. 153, spelling modernised).
3. *MB.*, vi. (339), 273. 'Et incontinenti coram cardinalibus et aliis lachrymatus est [rex], et dominus Willelmus cardinalis visus est lachrymari. Dominus Otho vix a cachinno se potuit abstinere.'

riposted with a papal letter re-imposing the ban unless they gave up the Canterbury lands they were holding. Finally, the legates inhibited the archbishop from any further excommunications, while Gilbert wrote in the name of the English Church to Alexander setting out his crimes.

Although there is no record of events at the papal court at this time, it is clear that envoys from both parties were harassing Alexander. He seems to have regretted his gentleness to Henry, for in May 1168 he commissioned Simon, prior of Mont Dieu, and Bernard de la Coudre to approach Henry with letters of warning that unless he came to terms with the archbishop dire consequences would follow; should they fail to make contact with him they must make sure that he receives the threatening letters they carry.[1] The documents at this point are difficult to date, but it would seem that nothing had happened by the end of the year, when the emissaries, with Englebert, prior of Val de S. Pierre, added to them, succeeded in getting king and archbishop near to each other at Montmirail on 6 January 1169, with the French king in the offing. Thomas was at last persuaded to approach the king, kneel before him and beg peace from him for the honour of God. Henry took exception to these last words on the ground that they implied that Thomas alone regarded the honour of God, whereas he did not. Furthermore, he would be perfectly satisfied if the archbishop would obey the customs that his predecessors had kept. To which Thomas replied that he would keep the customs *saving his order*.[2] This reservation, as the companions of the archbishop knew, would wreck all hopes of concord as it had done at Clarendon and at Northampton. They had done their best to persuade Thomas to make no conditions for the moment, but to remain silent and put himself at the king's disposition. It was a crucial moment, but Thomas stood firm. The two kings departed, Henry in anger, Louis with more sympathy for Henry than for Thomas. On this occasion all his household, including Herbert of Bosham, thought his action obstinate and unwise, and said so openly. John of Poitiers went so far as to accuse him of destroying the Church of God. 'Brother', replied the archbishop, 'have a care that the Church of God be not destroyed by

1. *MB.*, vi. (424), 438–440.
2. *MB.*, vi. (461), 506 ff.

you; by me, God willing, it shall never be destroyed'.[1] Earlier in
the day, even King Louis had asked him if he wished to be more
than a saint, and now he had left the meeting without a word of
friendship for Thomas.[2]

The two parties thus stood exactly as before, and the papal
emissaries, having served the pope's warning letter on the king,
could do no more. John of Canterbury, now bishop of Poitiers,
took on himself the part of go-between and suggested to Henry
that a meeting should take place without *parti pris* and the king
suggested that he should be at Tours and Thomas at Marmoutier.
The archbishop would have nothing of this. He could not arrive
at the conference as if his mind had changed. He would promise
anything, but *saving the honour of God and his order*. As he wrote to
the pope: 'If the customs he demands were to prevail, the authority
of the apostolic see in England would disappear altogether or be
reduced almost to nothing'. The pope need have no fear of a schism
with Henry. As for the customs, he did not know precisely what
these were now in the king's mind, and without the pope's
authority it would be wrong for him to alter the form of Church
government which the whole western Church accepted. Let the
pope act strongly. If he strikes fear into the godless, he will restore
peace to the Church.[3] Meanwhile, a second confrontation of the
two parties on 7 February had had exactly the same result as before,
but despite the strong support given to Thomas by his advocates,
the pope stalled, and on 28 February announced the appointment
once again of two legates. This was the result, it appears, of the
clever diplomacy of Reginald FitzJocelin and Ralph, archdeacon
of Llandaff. The two legates were again chosen to represent the
two opinions which still existed in the Curia—Gratian, a steady
friend of Thomas, and Vivian.[4] The archbishop, for his part, took
strong action again, and excommunicated Foliot on Palm Sunday,
13 April 1169, along with Jocelin of Salisbury, Randulph de Broc
and a group of those who had invaded or retained Canterbury
estates.[5] The letters of excommunication did not reach London till
Ascension Day, 29 May. Thomas's agent, a man of the name of

1. H. Bosham, *MB.*, iii. 428.
2. *MB.*, iii. 425.
3. *MB.*, vi. (466), 519–23.
4. *MB.*, vi. (476), 537–8.
5. *MB.*, vi. (479, 480, 488), 541–3; 558–9.

Berengarius, entered St Paul's Cathedral, where a Mass was in progress, and at the offertory approached the celebrant, who took him to be making an offering, and thrusting the letter of excommunication into his hand, bade him in the name of the pope and the archbishop to read the sentence out before continuing the Mass.[1] Foliot immediately called a meeting of the London clergy, and maintained, though greatly agitated, that the excommunication was invalid both because his case had never been impartially judged, and still more because the see of London was independent and not under the jurisdiction of the archbishop of Canterbury, to whom he had always, and successfully, refused to promise obedience.[2]

Gilbert's claim, of which this is the first known expression, that London had been, and should remain, a see independent of Canterbury, was for long treated by historians either as an invention, or an exaggeration, of his enemies, or as an endeavour to set up London as a third metropolitan see. Actually, whatever the source or motive of Foliot's proposal, it was clearly the transference of the metropolitan dignity from Canterbury to London, or, in Gilbert's mind, the restitution to London of the dignity that it once had, that was in question. Recent scholarship has pointed out that the claim, although canonically and historically baseless, had a slight foundation in fact, and a firmer one in legend.[3] London and not Canterbury had been a see in Roman Britain, and Gregory the Great certainly directed Augustine to found metropolitan churches at London and York. Actually, historical circumstances took charge; the pope acquiesced, and Canterbury became from the first the pivot of the southern portion of the hierarchy. But the story of London's ancient dignity survived, and Richard of Belmeis, whose family was related to the Foliots and whose relatives of the second generation were still members of the London chapter when Gilbert became bishop, had put forward a claim to independence on his election in 1108[4]. Since then, Geoffrey of Monmouth in his *History* had given metropolitan status in ancient times to York and London, and flimsy as this may seem as a reason for turning an established province upside down, we have been reminded that claims, genuine or bogus, to metropolitan rights were almost

1. W. FitzStephen, *MB.*, iii. 89. Cf. *MB.*, vi. (508), 603.
2. *MB.*, vi. (508), 605–6.
3. See long discussion in *GF.*, 151–62.
4. *GF.*, 157.

epidemic in the early twelfth century and at other times earlier. Besides the Canterbury-York dispute there was the claim of St David's to metropolitan status, and the more recent and even less reputable attempt of Henry of Winchester to secure the same rank for his see. Gilbert Foliot had steadfastly refused to pledge his obedience to the see of Canterbury when he was translated from Hereford. His ostensible reason, which was in fact allowed, was that he had already given his promise to Canterbury when elected to Hereford,[1] but the obstinacy with which he held to what, even if valid, appeared to contemporaries to be an ungracious and unnecessary protest, argued some ulterior motive. Many, at the time, found this in an unwillingness to submit in any way to the archbishop whose election he had opposed and whose person he disliked. This may well have been the deepest reason, but Gilbert also may have had the reputed ancient status of London in mind. There is the same ambiguity of motive in 1169, and here again, it is hard to avoid the supposition that it was bitter enmity, *non serviam*, that led to the production of the historical claim to independence.

In any case, though claiming to be covered also by his previous appeal, Gilbert was once more torn by claims of ecclesiastical obedience which were a part of his basic attitude to episcopal office, and he decided to act as if the excommunication were valid, whatever his professions to the contrary.[2] He was fairly in the toils, for the king expected him to disregard the sentence and would not allow him to approach the pope in person for justification or absolution. He, therefore, sent letters to Rome, and a group of friends all wrote testimonials on his behalf to Alexander, which were met by an equally impressive set of counter-testimonials from the archbishop's friends. Alexander, for his part, wrote to Thomas in June, criticising his censures and asking for their removal.

Meanwhile, John of Salisbury had met the legates at Vézelay on 22 July. One of them, Gratian, nephew of Eugenius III, was an old friend on whose sympathy for the archbishop he could trust.[3] A month later, Henry met the legates at Domfront, and received them politely, though their talk was interrupted by the arrival of Prince Henry and a group of hunters, all blowing horns to

1. *MB.*, v. (35), 56.
2. *MB.*, vi. (509) 607–10; *GFL.*, no. 204.
3. *MB.*, vii. (532), 2–3.

announce the killing of a stag. The next day the legates were faced with the king and his trusty agents, John, dean of Salisbury, Reginald FitzJocelin, and Ralph, archdeacon of Llandaff. Henry was in his most difficult mood and the meeting broke up in anger.[1] There was another meeting at Bures on 1 September, when another long wrangle took place, the king demanding absolution for his servants, and ultimately exclaiming: 'I know they will put an interdict on my realm, but cannot I, who can take a fortress a day, catch a clerk if he interdicts my land?' After prolonged negotiations, which moved from place to place, there was a breakdown once more on the insistence of both parties to accept any agreement with conditions added; on the king's part it was 'saving the dignity of my kingdom', and on the archbishop's 'saving the liberty of the Church'. Moreover, the king refused to give the kiss of peace. It was probably at this point that Gratian, despairing of Henry's good faith, retired from his commission and ultimately returned to Rome.[2]

It was in the autumn of 1169, also, that Henry decided to take more drastic action against the pope. He feared, with reason, that his realm might be placed under interdict, and wished to forestall this. There are several versions of the decrees, which sharpened and added to the Clarendon Constitutions. Anyone who brought into the country an interdict from the pope or the archbishop was to be treated as a traitor, and if anyone, cleric or lay, were to observe such an interdict, he was to be exiled with all his relations, and without any of their possessions. No one was to write to the pope or appeal to him or the archbishop, and no one was to leave England without permission. All who showed favour to the pope or archbishop were to suffer loss of all their possessions, and all clerics abroad who had rents in England were to return under pain of their confiscation. All entering the country were to be searched for letters and to present their passports. Finally, all over fifteen years old in town and country throughout England were to swear to an observance of all these decrees. Peter's Pence were to be collected as usual, but paid into the royal treasury.[3]

1. *MB.*, vii. (560), 70–3.
2. *MB.*, vii. (606), 161–3. Cf. H. Tillmann, *Die päpstlichen Legaten in England*, Bonn 1926, 66–7.
3. These decrees are given in *MB.*, vii. (599–600), 147 ff. and by William of Canterbury, *MB.*, i. 53–5, Gervase of Canterbury, i. 214–5 (who gives

These decrees, it would seem, were widely ignored and perhaps never fully implemented. They would seem to have been caught up by other events within a few months and partially ignored by all parties, though the coastal guard was maintained throughout 1170. But in themselves they aimed at a severance of links between England and the papacy almost as complete as that accomplished by the parliament of Henry VIII. They were to come into force on 9 October, and six weeks after that date yet another meeting was arranged between the king and the archbishop. This time the legate Vivian took the occasion of a meeting between Henry and King Louis at Montmartre, then outside the city of Paris. The meeting began without bargaining. Thomas petitioned Henry for the restoration of all rights and possessions to himself and his companions. All uncomfortable topics were avoided and the settlement, so far as it went, was on the point of execution when the archbishop asked of the king, as the only pledge of good faith he needed, a kiss of peace. This Henry refused to give, alleging an oath he had sworn in the past. After the conference even Vivian remarked that he could not recollect ever having seen or heard a greater liar than Henry.[1]

At long last Alexander III had had enough. On 19 January 1170, he commissioned archbishop Rotrou of Rouen and bishop Bernard of Nevers to carry matters to a conclusion from the meeting at Montmartre. Henry was to receive archbishop Thomas back into England and restore all his property, with a thousand marks added for him to set up house again. Thomas on his side was to offer full submission, saving the freedom of the church (*salva ecclesiae libertate*). If the king refused, an interdict was to be imposed. If the king submitted, then, after a decent pause, he was

---

the date, 9 October) and R. Hoveden, i. 231–3 (both in RS). Stubbs gives a useful note to the passage of Hoveden. Doubt has been expressed in the past as to the date and significance of these decrees but there can be no doubt that autumn 1169 is the true date, and that they aimed at the ecclesiastical isolation of England, at least as a temporary measure. See also letter of Thomas, *MB.*, vii. (636), 220–3 and John of Salisbury *ibid.* (641), 235 concerning the oath. William FitzStephen, *MB.*, iii. 102, describes the oath and mentions Thomas's letter of absolution (no. 636, cited above); other references are in *MB.*, vii. (593, 610, 650), 138, 175–6, 261.

1. *MB.*, vii. (609), 172. 'Rex ille prae cunctis mortalibus sophistice [i.e. untruthfully] vivit et loquitur.'

to be required to renounce the Constitutions. If he boggled, the commissioners and Thomas were to inform the pope. If things looked hopeful, the excommunicated persons were to be absolved —and to be re-excommunicated if things went ill. If the king would not give the kiss of peace, the archbishop was to be coaxed to accept a kiss from the young Henry. Failing this, they were to report back. Alexander wrote to Henry in the same sense, and to Foliot, to whom he promised absolution on condition of his acceptance of any further papal control.

Thomas for his part wrote (or caused another to write) to the bishop of Nevers giving him a short list of conditions to put to Henry, with warnings and detailed instructions how he might best deal with the shifty, treacherous and obstinate king, and with insistence that the kiss of peace must be given, and given in person.[1]

1. *MB.*, vii. (626), 204–9; (623), 198–202; (644), 246–7.

CHAPTER 9

Defiance and Reconciliation

ALL THESE plans were thrown into disarray by the news that King Henry was planning to have his son crowned in England while the archbishop was still abroad and unreconciled. Such a coronation, which had its remote precedent in the nomination by the Roman emperors of a successor who thenceforward bore some of the imperial titles, had been practised in the German empire and on occasion by the kings of France. It was in fact the common practice of designating a successor put to dynastic use. In England it was unknown, save for the recent attempt by King Stephen to crown his son Eustace, which had been frustrated by a papal prohibition at Theobald's request, largely through the diplomatic ability of Thomas himself fifteen years previously.[1] In Henry's case the desire had been of long standing, as we have seen, and had nearly come to fruition in 1161–2. When Alexander III renewed the traditional powers of the archbishop in 1166, the coronation of kings was once more reserved to Canterbury, and some time in 1169 Thomas had warned his envoy to the Curia of the enduring danger.[2] The new move on Henry's part may have been the outcome of the recent treaty of marriage between the fifteen-year-old Henry and the still younger daughter of King Louis, and it is worth remarking that the Emperor Frederick, a few months previously (15 August 1169) had crowned his son Henry as King of the Romans. Beyond this, there was the ever-present anxiety of the succession to the throne. Whatever the motive, it was a singularly unwise move. Although Henry had ruined more than one attempt at reconciliation with Thomas, he had hitherto consistently maintained that he desired a settlement, as had also the archbishop. It was, indeed, greatly to the interests of all

1. See above p. 26.
2. *MB.*, vii. (612), 181–2.

concerned, and of the Church and the country at large, that a reconciliation should take place. Now, quite gratuitously, Henry proposed to outrage the dignity of his opponent by the invasion of a clear and immemorial right, for the coronation was to be performed by the archbishop of York, already *persona non grata* with Thomas on more than one count.

The wrath of the archbishop immediately vented itself in letters to the hierarchy in England, including one to Roger of York, with a backhand reference to auld lang syne at Canterbury.[1] These letters were apparently written in March,[2] but there is no date to a letter of Alexander III brusquely forbidding the coronation and usually referred to a later date.[3] It is unfortunate that the absence of firm dating and erroneous arrangement of the correspondence make it difficult to reconstruct the sequence of events, which is crucial for any examination of this episode. Alexander, it must always be remembered, was now at Benevento or in its neighbourhood, which made it quite impossible for him to keep up with events in northern France and England.

In any case Thomas's distress was greatly increased by the permission, given by Alexander before the news of the coronation had reached him, for the absolution of Gilbert Foliot in England to remain secret and to be dependent on his observance of eventual papal instructions.[4] This happy indulgence, which seems to have been largely due to the diplomatic skill of Master David, Foliot's agent at the Curia, allowed the return of the bishop of London to England from Milan, whither he had struggled through the Alpes Maritimes to seek absolution from the pope, and on Easter Day, 1170, he was absolved. The secrecy was a farce; the news, spread by Gilbert himself, was in the papers, so to say, before Thomas had been informed.[5] His anguish is revealed in a series of letters in which the Curia is charged with venality and injustice. 'But', wrote the archbishop, 'with God's help I will never fail in faith to the Church, whether in life or in death. I am ready to die for her

1. *MB.*, vii. (651), 263–4.

2. *MB.*, vii. (651), 264. Thomas, appealing against the bishops, fixes the term at 2 February 1171. Normally, the term of an appeal was within a year of its announcement.

3. *MB.*, vii. (647), 256.

4. *MB.*, vii. (627), 208. Alexander's letter is dated 12 February 1170. For his conditions see *MB.*, vii. (655), 273.

5. *MB.*, vii. (658), 275–7.

SENS CATHEDRAL

The nave and apse of Sens, one of the earliest large churches to be completed in the new 'Gothic' style, were designed by William of Sens. The high altar was consecrated in 1164 and the fabric finished in 1168. *Studio Allix, Sens.*

liberty. But I can no longer trust in, or appeal to, Roman justice.'[1]
Ironically enough, in the great collection of letters on the controversy, Thomas's missive to the pope and Gilbert's effusive
letter of thanks are juxtaposed.[2]

When once the pope was seized of the possibility of an imminent
coronation, he acted decisively. On 24–26 February he despatched
letters to archbishop Thomas, Roger of York, and the other
bishops forbidding the coronation unless the king revoked the
Constitutions of Clarendon and the anti-papal oath which he had
exacted from his subjects, and unless the ceremony was then
performed by the archbishop of Canterbury.[3] These letters were
sent to Thomas for forwarding to England, and the archbishop,
having added a covering letter of his own, entrusted the whole
package to Roger of Worcester, then in Normandy, for instant
delivery to Roger of York and his colleagues.[4] In addition to his
public letters the archbishop commissioned a devout lady,
possibly a religious, to present a prohibitory missive in person to
Roger of York. This short letter is not without interest, as being
one of the very few in which the archbishop suits his style to the
recipient. Though written at a moment of crisis and passion, it
lacks entirely the strident note that sounds in many of Thomas's
letters. After reminding his trusted messenger of valiant women in
the Old Testament, he adds: 'The Mother of mercy will be with
you, she who brought forth Man and God to save the world. She
will ask her Son to be your guide, companion and protector.
Farewell, betrothed of Christ, and think of Him always as present'.[5]

It is impossible to be certain that any of these letters reached
their destination. They cannot have been despatched by Thomas
before mid-March, and on 3 March Henry had crossed the
Channel in great haste and in a storm that wrecked one of his
vessels.[6] Arrived in England, he strengthened the existing pre-
cautions against the introduction of papal letters or any kind of

1. *MB.*, vii. (662), 279–82 (especially pp. 280–1).
2. Thomas's letter is *MB.*, vii. (666), 292–4; Gilbert's *ibid.* (667),
295–8; *GFL.*, no. 212.
3. *MB.*, vii. (632–3), 216, 217.
4. *MB.*, vii. (649), 258–60.
5. *MB.*, vii. (672), 307. The date of this letter is uncertain. Can Idonea
be the daughter of Baldwin de Redvers (W. FitzStephen *MB.*, iii. 102)?
6. R. W. Eyton, *Court, Household and Itinerary of Henry II*, London
1878, 135.

communication from the archbishop. Roger of Worcester was forbidden by the king's agents from crossing the Channel.[1] FitzStephen, indeed, states that letters of prohibition reached the bishops of London and York on the eve of the coronation,[2] and this is borne out, with a covert reference to Roger of York, by an anonymous correspondent writing to the archbishop from England.[3] Herbert of Bosham likewise supports this in part.[4] On the other hand, Roger of York, more than a year later, as a condition for his absolution from censure, denied having ever seen the letter of prohibition.[5] In any case, apart altogether from the reports of the pope's action which must have been flying around in the three months before the ceremony, both Roger and the other bishops knew well enough not only of the tradition on the point, but of the explicit papal prohibition of 1166, and can scarcely have salved their consciences by inspecting the document of 1161 on which the king and Roger ostensibly relied.

The coronation duly took place with great display on 14 June at Westminster, Roger of York acting in the presence of Gilbert of London, Jocelin of Salisbury and almost all the English and Welsh bishops, with a few Norman prelates and a great gathering of barons. John of Salisbury advised instant action, and Thomas immediately wrote imposing an interdict on England within a fortnight though presumably the letter was not sent.[6] Henry knew well enough how serious his action had been, and immediately after the coronation[7] wrote from Westminster to Rotrou of Rouen, the

1. W. FitzStephen, *MB*., iii. 103.   2. *Ibid*.

3. *MB*., vii. (673), 309. 'Litterae domini papae super prohibitione consecrationis hujus diu est quod mare transierunt; sed inutiles prorsus effectae in manibus illius cui traditae sunt perierunt, nec alicui ostensae nec ullatenus propalatae.' Were these letters those of 26 February (*MB*., vii. (632–3), 216–7) or the undated letter of vii. (647), 256? Once again the order of these numbers is doubtful.

4. H. Bosham, *MB*., iii. 459. 'Et directas has sibi litteras quidam episcoporum ante coronationem receperunt.' On the other hand a friend writing to Thomas blames him: 'qui litteras non misistis quae poterant consecrationem impedire' (*MB*., vii. (676), 317).

5. *MB*., vii. (764), 502. 'Quod literas domini papae . . . nec recepit nec vidit nec aliquid fieri fecit quominus eas videret vel reciperet.'

6. *MB*., vii. (678), 320.

7. The coronation took place at Westminster on 14 June. On or about 24 June Henry embarked at Portsmouth (R. W. Eyton, *Court, Household and Itinerary of Henry II*, London 1878, 138).

legate, expressing his willingness to come to an agreement with
Thomas within the terms of the pope's instructions.[1] Crossing to
Normandy, he was visited by the legates Rotrou and Bernard, who
had themselves been about to cross to England, and, after hearing
the papal terms, agreed to all save the kiss of peace. A few days
later he met the king of France near La Ferté, and Thomas,
though unwilling at first, was persuaded (16 July) by the archbishop of Sens to accompany him and the legates to a meeting at
Fréteval (22 July). A long letter from Thomas to the pope gives an
account of the meeting. The king, as soon as the archbishop came
in sight, leapt forward to greet him. He was, so Thomas writes (was
he once more, after all these sad years, caught by the old enchant-
ment of the *faux bonhomme*?) a new man, and they talked together
as if no ruffle had ever disturbed their friendship. Henry promised
amendment and the punishment of evil counsellors, and declared
himself convinced by Thomas's historical proof of the claims of
Canterbury. The talk ended with gestures of mutual submission,
and the archbishop of Sens arranged the final concord. No mention
was to be made of the Constitutions, none of the restoration of
property. All was to be settled later. Another long conversation
then took place, as in olden days, and another meeting was fixed for
the near future before Thomas returned to England. The archbishop did not press for the kiss of peace, as Henry still held up his
scruple to break the oath he had sworn that it should never be
given.[2] It was, perhaps, the only oath he never broke. The archbishop's change of tone, following upon the years of stubborn
fencing and Thomas's clear-sighted *aide mémoire* composed only
a few months previously, setting out the conditions of agreement
and warning again and again against Henry's duplicity,[3] is
extremely difficult to understand. More than once in the past
Thomas, without consulting his friends, had taken a sudden resolve,
it might be either of acquiescence in, or resistance to, the king's
will. Had the old fascination for Henry surged up irresistibly in one
who had for six years kept all his emotions at bay? Or, like
Gregory at Canossa, did he choose open-eyed to accept the
proposed act of reconciliation in simple faith as a father in God, be

1. *MB.*, vii. (669), 300.
2. *MB.*, vii. (684), 326–38; cf. p. 339. 'Huic [osculo] publice in conspectu
Francorum apud Montem Martyrum abjuraverat.'
3. *MB.*, vii. (610), 173–9.

the outcome what it might? Or did he decide that there was no way out but one, and that he must dree his weird?

In any case, peace had been established, and Henry ratified it in writing, though with the significant words 'saving the honour of my kingdom'. Thomas was not wholly satisfied, but willing to think that his repeated assertion that nothing but a serious threat would move the king had been a correct estimate.[1] The pope for his part begged pardon of the archbishop for his ambiguous diplomacy, which he attributed to his fear of causing a schism. Now, by way of amends, he provided a blanket censure for Roger of York, the bishops of London, Salisbury, Exeter, Chester, Llandaff, St Asaph and Geoffrey Ridel.[2] Thomas was also the recipient of many curial comments. Some of the cardinals were not optimistic; thus, cardinal Albert wrote that the leopard could not change his spots.[3] On 9 October Alexander felt obliged to depute the archbishops of Sens and Rouen to visit the king and command him to implement his promises, adding to them a revocation of the 'cursed Constitutions'.[4] The threat of an interdict was once more laid upon the king. Four days later the pope authorised Thomas to re-impose the censures if the reconciliation went sour. A little later Thomas wrote what was perhaps his noblest letter to the pope. He has received, he says, Alexander's letters of excommunication, but he begs for permission to withhold them, even those against Gilbert of London, if there is prospect of a settlement. Roger of York alone, the mover and cause of all this evil, is reserved for papal judgment. He would prefer to lose by gentleness than harm the Church in England by violence. He intends to go to England, whether peace or suffering is before him. What God has decreed will come to pass, whatever it be. He ends with a request for prayers and a dignified word of gratitude to the pope for all his help.[5]

The shadows were, indeed, falling round him. Early in October the agents he had sent to England reported that the restoration of property had been postponed, and that though most men longed for his return they feared the royal officials. Nor did Henry inspire confidence. When Thomas arrived at Tours, where Henry was

---

1. *MB.*, vii. (695), 351–3.
2. *MB.*, vii. (699), 357–9.
3. *MB.*, vii. (703), 369. 'Non facile mutat . . . pardus varietates suas.'
4. *MB.*, vii. (710), 376–7.
5. *MB.*, vii. (716), 384–9. For Roger see p. 387.

meeting Theobald, Count of Blois, the king was cold and did not call upon him. The next morning, when arrangements were being made for Mass, Henry arranged for a *Requiem* Mass for the dead, in which the prayer for peace is omitted, to be said in his chapel in case the archbishop should assist, with the hope of exchanging the kiss of peace.[1]

Nevertheless, Thomas showed his old diplomatic adroitness, but the king would not agree to an immediate restoration of his property. It was on this occasion, when the two met near Tours, that the king was more friendly, and the old relationship seemed to be restored. 'Oh,' said Henry, 'why will you not do what I want? I would hand over everything to you then.' When the archbishop told Herbert of Bosham of this he added: 'and when the king used these words I remembered the words of the Gospel: "All these things will I give thee".'[2] When Thomas parted from Henry he said: 'My Lord, my heart tells me that I depart as one whom you will not see again'. 'Do you count me faithless, then?' asked the king. 'May you never be, my Lord' answered Thomas.[3]

There was worse news still to come. Roger of York, Gilbert Foliot and Jocelin of Salisbury had been summoned over to Normandy to advise the king as to the filling of the many vacant sees. This was another studied insult to the archbishop on a vital issue where Clarendon conflicted with canon law. John of Salisbury, sent on ahead to Canterbury, had found lands and churches still despoiled. Thomas complained bitterly to the king of the depredations of Randulph de Broc on Canterbury property.[4] Finally, a curt letter informed him that Henry could not meet him as arranged, at Rouen, for a journey to England together, but he had sent John of Oxford (of all people) to bear him company on the homeward journey. Yet Thomas, negligent as Caesar of the omens, though hearing that his enemies were robbing his estates and holding on to his churches, decided to cross the Channel. On 3 November, six years to the day from his arrival as an exile at Gravelines, he left Sens.[5]

1. H. Bosham, *MB.*, iii. 469.
2. *MB.*, iii. 470; cf. Anonymous I, *MB.*, iv. 67.
3. W. FitzStephen, *MB.*, iii. 116. Herbert and FitzStephen disagree as to what events took place at Tours and what at Amboise.
4. *MB.*, vii. (718), 394. John's letter is *ibid.*, (724), 407 ff.
5. Anonymous I, *MB.*, iv. 68.

K

Consistent always in his love of splendour, the archbishop started for the coast with a following of a hundred horsemen. Arrived at Witsand, he sent ahead by a boy named Osbern the papal excommunication of the bishops who had taken part in the coronation, in particular those of York, London and Salisbury. The boy met these three at Dover, where they were waiting to embark on their way to the king.[1]

While the archbishop was walking on the beach at Witsand judging the weather, the dean of Boulogne met him with a warning that the English coast was watched by his enemies. He had another warning from the master of a ship that had just crossed from England. He was going into the midst of his enemies who would certainly use violence. Thomas himself decided to change course from Dover, where the three bishops had a retinue of knights, to Sandwich a port on his own lands.[2] Even there his party was saved from attack only by the energetic action of John of Oxford. A crowd of poor folk were on shore, and sighting the archbishop's cross in one of the ships they ran into the water to get his blessing.[3]

1. Anonymous I, *MB.*, iv. 68, gives the boy's name as Osbern.
2. *Ibid.*
3. H. Bosham, *MB.*, iii. 477–8.

CHAPTER 10

The Return to Canterbury

THE RETURN of the archbishop was marked by scenes of rejoicing and omens of disaster. The beach at Sandwich had been crowded and the road to Canterbury was lined at intervals by groups of parishioners led by their priest. The citizens of Canterbury turned out in force to welcome the archbishop whom they had not seen for six years, and in his short stay Thomas confirmed large numbers of children, dismounting from his horse for the laying on of hands. Besides the satisfaction of having the primate of the Church in England back again amongst his own people, many of whom had known him for twenty years, it seems certain that his long exile endured for his opposition to the king had won for him in the minds of the people something of the appeal of a champion and a patriot. The reforms, fiscal and judicial, of Henry II and the firm control with which he held the country by means of his ministers, his justices, and his recently purged body of sheriffs, though to our eyes achievements of lasting value for the future of English law and administration, were to those who bore the brunt of the exactions the work of a harsh ruler and his myrmidons. We can appreciate that to the king who heard of what was happening, and still more to those who had for years occupied the Canterbury estates, the tumultuous welcome accorded to the archbishop, and his triumphal progress to London, might seem a potential threat to the royal power. To Thomas, on the other hand, the surly opposition and vicious attacks of Randulph de Broc and others, and the flight overseas to the king of Geoffrey Ridel, archdeacon of Canterbury, and of Richard of Ilchester, followed by that of the archbishop of York and the bishops of London and Salisbury, together with the knowledge that Henry intended with their advice to fill the six long vacant sees, clearly portended a return in England to a still more bitter and seemingly endless struggle against evil and faithlessness in high places.

Thomas arrived at Canterbury on 2 December. He was received by a great and jubilant crowd who, according to Bosham, threw their clothing on the road and cried: 'Blessed is he who comes in the name of the Lord'. Bells were rung and hymns sung. Thomas, his face flushed and triumphant, received the kiss of greeting from the whole community of monks, and the day was spent in rejoicing and feasting.[1] On Ember Saturday he held an ordination, and in chapter before Christmas he relaxed his ban against those who had been irregularly admitted into the community without his authority.

On the morrow of his arrival at Canterbury he was visited by two sets of envoys.[2] One came from the three bishops who had received the papal letters of censure a few days previously at Dover; they demanded absolution from their censures. They were supported by the royal officials, who urged that the censures that the archbishop had imposed were against the king's laws. To both Thomas gave the reply that was often to be repeated in the coming weeks. He had, he said, indeed asked the pope to excommunicate the offenders, but the censure when it came was the pope's, not his, and he could not act against it. He was willing to remit his own pronouncements of excommunication against Gilbert and Jocelin, and even now he was willing to grant absolution to the two bishops, if they would promise to abide by the pope's further decisions. As for Roger, Alexander III had specifically reserved to himself any relaxation of sentence. To this the servants of Henry replied that all the sentences were unlawful according to the custom of the realm. As for the bishops, there is evidence that they were willing to submit, but were overborne by Roger of York, who is said to have declared that he had wealth enough to deal with both pope and king. The bishops, therefore, having sent ahead by letter their account of the affair, decided to cross to Normandy at almost the same time as the king's men, Geoffrey Ridel and Richard of Ilchester.

Meanwhile, Thomas, after a week at Canterbury, sent messengers to the young king deprecating any suggestion of hostility

1 H. Bosham, *MB.*, iii. 479.
2. W. FitzStephen, *MB.*, iii. 120. Thomas's own accoun t is in a letter to Alexander III (vii. (723), 401–7).

and announcing his intention of visiting him at Winchester. He
started out to go by way of London, and true to his old self, he
conjured up three warhorses, handsome, majestic animals, high-
spirited thoroughbreds prancing and cavorting, with flowered and
parti-coloured trappings, as presents for his former ward.[1]
Walter of Rochester came out to greet him with a procession, and
from London a great crowd came three miles out of the city to
meet him and escort him to the church of the canons at Southwark.
With them came the scholars and clerks of the London churches,
singing the *Te Deum*. The archbishop, greatly moved, distributed
largesse, and when he arrived at the lodgings of the bishop of
Winchester the canons of Southwark and clergy greeted him with
the *Benedictus* and other hymns.

His envoy, prior Richard of Dover, found the young king at
Winchester, where a party had been collected of representatives of
the vacant sees who were about to cross to Normandy to meet the
king and elect his nominees to the bishoprics of Bath and Wells,
Chichester, Ely, Hereford, Lincoln and Carlisle. When Richard
arrived, the young king's guardians put up difficulties, and the
prior was sent back with the message that the archbishop would
hear from the young Henry later.[2] Forthwith two knights were sent
to Southwark with the message that he was to return to Canterbury
and not to travel about. Nevertheless, Thomas arranged that his
grievances should be put before the officials at the young king's
court.[3] The clergy, Thomas declared, were tried and punished by
the secular courts, the confiscated Canterbury property had not
been returned, nor had the churches, uncanonically filled with
priests and unlawfully held. Access to the pope was also prohibited.
To these general grievances were added a succession of small
insults. Robert de Broc had seized wine destined for the archbishop; a relative of his had docked the tail of a Canterbury horse
drawing provisions for the archbishop; the family group of Broc
was still occupying the archbishop's castle of Saltwood, and the
king's men were arresting the Canterbury tenants, poaching the
archbishop's game, and stealing his hounds. Thomas, himself,
when going to London and returning, had accepted a small escort
of knights, as there were rumours that he would be attacked, and

1. W. FitzStephen, *MB.*, iii. 122.
2. William of Canterbury, *MB.*, i. 105–112.
3. *MB.*, i. 112–3, 115–9.

this was repeated to King Henry in an inflated form, as if Thomas was organising a private army.[1]

Clearly matters were moving to a crisis. So long as both king and archbishop were out of England, conferences might fail and spiritual censures threaten without great harm to anyone, but now the king was abroad, while the archbishop was striking out right and left at his enemies, while he evoked from the people a welcome that was at least partly a sign of the popular approval of his resistance to the king, and which was certainly an exhibition of support such as no subject had received in England since the Norman Conquest. Granted that the king had only himself to thank for his unpopularity, both by his overbearing pressure on his subjects at home, and by his refusal to make a sincere move towards a compromise with his archbishop, yet Henry and his entourage may well have persuaded themselves that the archbishop was the centre of disaffection in England, behaving as if he had no master, excommunicating his personal enemies, including several of the king's servants, and that there was no knowing what he might do next. It is easy to reconstruct the picture painted by the king's men and the three bishops. Indeed, it was true that if the king remained immovable in his stand by the ancestral customs as established at Clarendon, a complete impasse had once more been reached, with the difference that now Thomas was back in his cathedral with the spiritual arm of the papacy behind him. If neither party would yield, some kind of violence must take over. Both Thomas and Henry knew this. At their last meeting the archbishop had told the king that he would never see him again, and he gave the solemn warning to his clerks at Canterbury and to his people in the cathedral that the contest could not end without bloodshed and that Alphege, murdered by the Danes, would have a successor at Canterbury.[2]

On Christmas Day, which fell on a Friday, Thomas preached to the crowds in the cathedral, warning them that they would soon lose their pastor. He then excommunicated once more by name those who held Canterbury lands and churches unlawfully. On the following day he sent Herbert of Bosham and Alexander Llewellyn to report to the king of France how matters stood, though his real motive may well have been to save his two most outspoken

1. W. FitzStephen, *MB.*, iii. 124.
2. *MB.*, iii. 130.

companions, the constant advisers of resistance, out of reach of the king's vengeance. To Herbert, as to Henry, he bade a last farewell.[1]

Meanwhile, at Bures, near Bayeux, where Henry was spending Christmas, anger against the archbishop was mounting. The tidings of Thomas's arrival at Canterbury had been followed by the letters of the excommunicated prelates; these were followed up by the arrival of the king's servants and the bishops themselves. The manor house in which the king lay was an old property of the dukes of Normandy, and tradition or legend had it that in the chamber there Harold had taken the fatal oath that gave the crown of England to William. There, on Christmas Eve, it seems that Henry took the decision with his barons that the archbishop must be silenced.[2] The earl of Essex and others were despatched to England; the young king's tutors were to go to Canterbury with an armed force; the coasts on both sides of the Channel were to be watched in case Thomas once more attempted to escape. The archbishop was either to be imprisoned or confined to his quarters at Canterbury until he consented to remove all censures from his opponents.[3]

All these plans were set in train and the coast of Kent was ringed with armed groups, but we can only guess what might have happened had not unofficial action brought about a decision. What exactly was said by the king and others is uncertain. One biographer attributes the immediate blame to Roger of York, who told Henry bluntly that he would never have peace while Thomas lived. Another states that the king in fury kept girding at those around him: 'What a set of idle cowards I keep in my kingdom who allow me to be mocked so shamefully by a low-born clerk'.[4] Words like this were certainly thrown about, as the king himself admitted, and four of his household met together and swore to avenge the king. They were not, as has sometimes been said, lesser knights of his company, but barons of substance, 'barons of

1. H. Bosham, *MB.*, iii. 486.
2. Bur' is named by H. Bosham, *MB.*, iii. 481 and *GW.*, lines 5042, 5096–5100. It is generally agreed that this is Bures (Calvados, arr. Caen). Guernes has the folklore about Harold.
3. Cf. W. FitzStephen, *MB.*, iii. 129. Accounts differ as to whether the knights set off two days before Christmas *before* the king's decision to move against the archbishop, or on the night of 24–5 December after the king's council.
4. Anonymous I, *MB.*, iv. 69; William of Canterbury, *MB.*, i. 122. *GW.*, lines 5126–33 accuses Roger.

his household, magnates of substance, notable even among his great men'.[1] Hugh of Moreville had witnessed at Clarendon; in this very year of 1170 he had been an itinerant justice in Northumberland and Durham; he had large estates in the North centred upon Knaresborough. William de Tracy had lands in Gloucester, Somerset and Devon. Reginald FitzUrse was a son of Richard FitzUrse and Sibylla, grand-niece of Henry I. Richard le Breton had lands in Somerset.[2]

They left the court secretly, and when they were missed a vain attempt was made to overtake them. Travelling rapidly and separately, they found wind and tide in their favour and arrived almost simultaneously at Saltwood Castle, which held a garrison under Randulph de Broc. There, on the night of Innocent's Day, they planned what they were to do on the morrow, making use of the detachments of knights and men-at-arms who had already been alerted by commands from the king in France.[3] It is not absolutely clear that murder was on the agenda at Saltwood that night. The utterances of the knights at Canterbury in the archbishop's hall, and the declarations of some of them after the catastrophe imply that their prime object, failing a lifting of the excommunications and other conditions, was to take the archbishop captive, and that they only turned to murder when thrown off their balance by the archbishop's resistance and the hostile crowd in the church. On the other hand, one of them at least admitted that their original plan was to strike the archbishop down in his private room next to the hall.[4] In any case, they were men of violence and in their plans, such as they were, they had probably made allowance for accidents.

The afternoon of 29 December 1170, at Canterbury, was covered by a group of competent reporters more completely than any other moment of medieval history. Nine biographers, all men of learning and standing, four of whom were present at the martyrdom, describe it in detail, and it is mentioned also by several contemporary historians.[5] There is some disagreement, real or apparent,

1. H. Bosham, *MB.*, iii. 487.
2. *D.N.B.*, *s. vv.*, and *GW.*, pp. 295–8.
3. William of Canterbury, *MB.*, i. 127; W. FitzStephen, *MB.*, iii. 131–2.
4. See below p. 142.
5. The four present were John of Salisbury, William of Canterbury, William FitzStephen and Edward Grim. It is difficult, sometimes impossible, in the martyrdom narrative to decide between two conflicting

on details, as there is in the Gospel narratives of the Passion of Christ, which afford an interesting literary parallel, but in the one case as in the other the differences are such as would be inevitable in the circumstances of rapid action by shifting groups and individuals, and serve rather to show the basic reliability and honesty of the writers. It is wholly characteristic of medieval biographers that they should borrow heavily from each other while retaining details of individual experience, and should make no attempt to iron out discrepancies. The account of Edward Grim, the clerk from Cambridge who had come to Canterbury a few days previously to see the great archbishop, is perhaps the most reliable.[1]

On Tuesday, 29 December, the archbishop had made his customary round of the altars of the cathedral, praying to the saints of their dedication, and making his confession to Thomas of Maidstone. He then joined his household at dinner in the hall, and retired afterwards to the large inner room where he worked and slept, accompanied by a number of his companions, among whom was John of Salisbury. The four knights arrived about three o'clock in the afternoon.[2] They entered the great court with Robert de Broc, a clerk and nephew of Randulph, who had been in charge of the place during the absence of the archbishop. They had left the bulk of their force outside the great gate, to prevent any of the citizens from entering and to keep the archbishop and his people from escaping. William FitzNeal, the archbishop's unfaithful seneschal, led them into the great hall, where the servers were at their meal.[3] Refusing an invitation to join them, the knights, conducted by the seneschal, announced their arrival from the king to the archbishop. Bidden to enter, they sat in silence without saluting Thomas or he them.[4] At last, looking at them intently, he greeted them; all remained silent save FitzUrse, who

---

accounts of details. In the narrative that follows, every statement has contemporary authority, but contradictory versions have been dropped without notice.

1. This is the opinion also of D. C. Douglas, who gives an excellent selection in *EHD.*, ii. 761–9.
2. W. FitzStephen, *MB.*, iii. 132 'hora quasi decima' (c. 2.40 p.m.); Anonymous I, *MB.*, iv. 70, 'circa horam nonam' (2 p.m.); Benedict of Peterborough, ii. 1 'circa horam diei undecimam' (3.20 p.m.).
3. Anonymous I, *MB.*, iv. 70; W. FitzStephen, iii. 132.
4. W. FitzStephen, *MB.*, iii. 132; E. Grim, *MB.*, ii. 430.

growled: 'God help you'.[1] Thomas flushed scarlet at the insult. 'We have a message for you from the king', said FitzUrse. 'Will you hear it in public or private?' 'As you will', replied the archbishop, and the monks and clerks began to go out. Then, changing his mind, Thomas called them back. The knights said later that had they been left alone with the archbishop they would have brained him with the haft of the cross that stood by his chair.[2] When the company had returned, FitzUrse accused him from the king of not absolving the clerks and bishops whom he had excommunicated. 'The sentence was not mine, but the pope's.' 'You were behind it.' 'Granted, but the sentence itself was given by one greater than I. Let those concerned go to the pope for absolution.' 'The king's command is that you and yours shall leave his realm; there can be no peace with you after your insolence.' 'Stop your threats, Reginald. I trust in the Lord of heaven. I tell you, that at Fréteval the king gave me his peace and safe-conduct. I did not return to flee again. Anyone who wants me can find me here.' 'I am telling you what the king says. You have been mad enough to excommunicate his officers.' Here the archbishop stood up. 'I will strike anyone', he replied, 'who violates the right of the Roman see or the Church of Christ.' At this the knights moved towards him, exclaiming: 'You have spoken at peril of your life.' 'Have you come to kill me?', asked Thomas, 'I commit myself and my cause to the Judge of all men. Your swords are less ready to strike than is my spirit for martyrdom. Find someone else to fly from you. Me you will find foot against foot in the Lord's fight.[3] I fled once from my post; I returned at the pope's counsel and command. If I am allowed to carry on my priestly duties, well and good. If not, God's will be done. But as for you, remember that you are my liege men.'[4]

1. Anonymous I, *MB.*, iv. 71. 'fertur tamen Rainaldus filius Ursionis quasi ex contemptu dicere: "Deus te adjuvet" '. E. Grim, ii. 431, has 'Et ficte ut [other MSS have 'ut ficte' and 'ut sic te'] Deus illum adjuvet imprecati sunt. Ad quod verbum ... vir Dei incredibili rubore perfunditur.' The dialogue in the text is conflated from several reports.
2. Anonymous I, *MB.*, iv. 71.
3. E. Grim, *MB.*, ii. 433. 'Me enim pede ad pedem in praelio Domini reperietis.' W. FitzStephen, *MB.*, iii. 134 has the same words. Both were present.
4. W. FitzStephen, *MB.*, iii. 135. 'Hoc autem dicebat commemorans quod Raginaldus ... et Willelmus ... et Hugo ..., dum adhuc cancellarius erat, propria deditione homines facti sunt ... quisque eorum ipsius jus imperiumque susceperat, genibus minor [i.e. kneeling].'

'We are the king's men, and renounce our fealty to you', and FitzUrse added: 'we can do more than threaten.' By this time voices had risen on both sides, and those in the hall had crowded round the door of the inner room. FitzUrse cried out to them that if they were loyal servants of the king, let them abandon the archbishop. Then, when no one moved, he added: 'We bid you guard this fellow. Let him not escape.' Then, as they turned to go, the archbishop strode to the door and shouted at them. 'You will find me here, I tell you, here.' And he struck his head with his hand.[1]

The knights pushed their way through the press in the hall and out through the main door, dragging with them some of the archbishop's men, crying out 'To arms, men, to arms.' The cry was heard by their followers in a house across the road, and they poured into the great court, shouting 'King's men, king's men, king's men.' The regular doorkeeper was dragged away and the gate shut once more to prevent help from outside coming in.

Meanwhile Thomas had turned back from the door of his room and sat down on his bed. There was an animated discussion as to what had been said on both sides. Some said the knights were drunk[2], others that the archbishop was safe with the king's peace. Anyway, it was Christmas, the season of peace and mercy. John of Salisbury, who had interrupted the dialogue with FitzUrse, begging the archbishop to discuss calmly with the knights the agreement with Henry at Fréteval, now returned to the subject. 'You are doing what you always do. You act and speak just as you think best, without asking anyone's advice.' 'Well, master John,' replied Thomas, 'what would you wish done?' 'You ought to have called a meeting of your council. Those knights want nothing more than a good reason for killing you.' 'We have all got to die', said the archbishop, 'and we must not swerve from justice from fear of

1. E. Grim, *MB.*, ii. 433.
2. W. FitzStephen, *MB.*, iii. 137. In a lecture, 'Archbishop Thomas Becket: a character study' (reprinted in Knowles, *The Historian and Character*, Cambridge 1963, 98–128) delivered in 1949 I suggested that T. S. Eliot, in his play, *Murder in the Cathedral*, had unwittingly given currency to the view that the knights were drunk. Some years later I had a letter from Mr Eliot saying that he had not meant to give this impression, and regretted that actors had sometimes misinterpreted his intention by giving an appearance of drunkenness.

death. I am more ready to meet death for justice sake and for the Church of God than they are to inflict it on me.' 'We're sinners, the rest of us', said John, 'and not yet ready to die. I can't think of anyone except yourself who is asking for death at the moment.' 'May God's will be done', said Thomas quietly.[1]

Meanwhile, the knights had made ready in the great court. They had entered the archbishop's hall with cloaks over their coats of mail; these they now slung over the drooping branches of a mulberry tree and put on their hauberks.[2] FitzUrse compelled one of the archbishop's men to help him. They then made a rush for the door of the hall, but Osbert and Algar, servants of the archbishop, had bolted it firmly. Robert de Broc, who knew the site well, bade them follow him round the kitchen and through some bushes into the orchard on the south side of the hall. Here there was an outside stair[3], leading to a door from which there was access to the hall. The stairs were being repaired and the workmen—'as they always do', remarked William of Canterbury[4]—had knocked off for the day leaving their tools and a ladder lying about. Broc went up the ladder, followed by the knights who picked up axes and hatchets, and with these they broke through the shutters of a window and got into the hall, where they opened the door for their companions outside.

The din of the axes and the cracking woodwork, the shouting of the servants as they escaped down a staircase towards the cloister, added to the shrieks and cries of the townspeople who were being hustled by armed men at the west door of the cathedral, were borne into the room where the archbishop sat. His companions tried to make him move, but he refused. The monks who were present urged him to go into the cathedral. 'Not a bit of it. Don't

1. Anonymous I, *MB.*, iv. 74.
2. William of Canterbury, *MB.*, i. 130. 'Sub moro ramosa'.
3. For the route taken by the knights see sketch plan (p. 145) based on that of W. Urry. Several of the biographers give names and vivid details, e.g., William of Canterbury, *MB.*, i. 130-1; E. Grim, *MB.*, ii. 433-4; W. FitzStephen, *MB.*, iii. 163-7. *G.W.*, line 5401, supplies the word *oriol* (= oriel), for which the *New English Dictionary* gives among other meanings an outside stair leading to a window (cf. Benedict of Peterborough, *MB.*, ii. 10).
4. William of Canterbury, *MB.*, i. 130. 'Ubi architecti (sicut fit) ad necessaria digressi ferramenta sua reliquerant'.

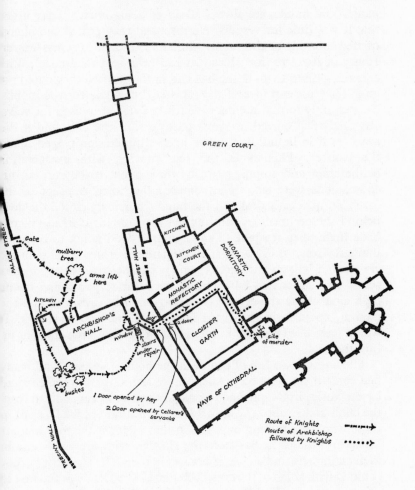

GREEN COURT

PALACE STREET

Gate

mulberry
tree

arms left
here

KITCHEN

GUEST HALL

KITCHEN

KITCHEN
COURT

MONASTIC
DORMITORY

MONASTIC
REFECTORY

ARCHBISHOP'S
HALL

door

window

2 door

stairs
under
repair

CLOISTER
GARTH

site
of murder

bushes

NAVE OF CATHEDRAL

PRECINCT WALL

1 Door opened by key

2 Door opened by Cellarer's
servants

Route of Knights

Route of Archbishop
followed by Knights

CANTERBURY

PLAN OF MONASTIC BUILDINGS
29 December 1170

Based with permission on the plan by Dr. W. Urry in
Canterbury under the Angevin Kings. VOL. II

panic. You monks are always afraid of being hurt.'[1] They urged that it was time for vespers. He rose, and they pulled and almost carried him out of the room, while he called to his cross-bearer Henry of Auxerre (for Alexander had been sent to France). With enemies behind them in the hall and in the orchard they dared not go to the west entrance of the minster, but made for the monks' cloister, only to find the door, which had not been used for years seemingly fast barred. A monk tried to shift the bolt, and it slid away 'as if in liquid glue'.[2] The hurried procession passed round the cloister, Thomas at the rear moving with exasperating deliberation and stopping two or three times to be sure all his companions were safe. They entered the north transept of the early Norman cathedral and the monks hurriedly closed the door behind the archbishop, shutting out some of his clerks. Thomas bade them open it again. 'The Church of God is not to be made into a fortress.' A cry was raised: 'There are armed knights in the cloister!' 'I will go and meet them', said Thomas, but the monks seized him again and bore him towards the steps leading to the high altar above the crypt. The short day had drawn in and the church, apart from the ritual lamps and candles, was dark. It would have been easy for him to escape either into the crypt or up into the roof.

The church was full of people at the hour of vespers, and many had come there alarmed by the sight of armed men in the city and by the noises in the precinct. Some of the monks came down from the choir and swelled the crowd. The archbishop broke loose from those who were pulling him, and at that moment the four knights broke into the cathedral from the cloister, with drawn swords in their right hand and an axe or hatchet in their left. In the dusk they collided with some of the crowd; Reginald FitzUrse was the first to enter, bawling; 'Hither to me, king's men! Where is Thomas Beketh, traitor to the king and the kingdom?'[3] Thomas, who had begun to climb the steps, turned and came down, while the three other knights and a body of men-at-arms from the local garrisons

1. W. FitzStephen, *MB.*, iii. 138. 'Plerique monachi plus justo timidi sunt et pusillanimes'. But one at least remained by Thomas.
2. E. Grim, *MB.*, ii. 435. 'Ac si glutino cohaesisset'.
3. *MB.*, ii. 435, ' "Ubi est Thomas Beketh, proditor regis et regni?" ' This is the only occurrence of the name in the Lives, and is used insultingly.

entered the church. 'Here am I; no traitor but a priest and an archbishop', and he took his stand by the east wall of the north transept, by a pillar of the arcading. His archiepiscopal cross was on his left, held now by Grim; on his right the altar of St Benedict, and facing him at the east end of the transept a statue of the Blessed Virgin above her altar against the north wall. Once more the knights demanded absolution for those whom Thomas had excommunicated; once more the archbishop refused. 'I am ready for you here', he said, 'but let my people go free.' At this his clerks, John of Salisbury among them, left him and took refuge in dark corners or under altars. Only Robert of Merton, William Fitz-Stephen and Edward Grim stood by him, though one or two monks were nearby. A clerk named Hugh Mauclerc, who had come with the knights, shouted: 'Absolve the bishops!' 'I have told you I will not change my mind.' At this the knights made a rush at him and tried to hoist him on to the back of William Tracy, with the object of taking him out of the church either to kill him or to bind him prisoner. The archbishop resisted, and Grim, with his arms round Thomas, helped him to shake them off. Then FitzUrse came at him. 'Reginald, Reginald', said Thomas, 'is this your return for all my gifts to you? Do you bear a sword against me?'[1] FitzUrse gripped his cloak. 'Hands off, Reginald, you pander', exclaimed Thomas[2] and sent the knight reeling back. Two others rushed in, one striking him on the shoulders with the flat of his sword, and hitting one of the monks.[3] Thomas bent forward covering his eyes with his hands, and they heard him say: 'To God and blessed Mary, Denis and Alphege, I commend myself.' FitzUrse, furious from his first encounter, now struck at his head, knocking off his fur cap and cutting off the top of his scalp. The sword fell on Thomas's left shoulder, cutting through all his clothes to the skin. Edward Grim, with his arms round the archbishop, had seen the blow coming and held out his arm to ward it off. His arm was deeply cut and the bones broken, and Grim fell away.[4] Thomas put his hand to his

1. William of Canterbury, *MB.*, i. 133. 'Reginalde, Reginalde, multa tibi contuli beneficia. Ingrederis armatus ad me?' Had Thomas in mind the rhythm of the Good Friday *Reproaches*? Cf. also E. Grim, *MB.*, ii. 436.

2. E. Grim, *MB.*, ii. 436. 'A se repulit, lenonem appellans'.

3. William of Canterbury, *MB.*, i. 134. 'Sed et unus ex fratribus circa patrem studio compassionis obversatus ictum pertulit.'

4. E. Grim, *MB.*, ii. 437. 'inter ulnas complexum tenuit [archiepiscopum]'.

head, saw the blood and said: 'Into thy hands, O Lord, I commit my spirit.'[1] Tracy struck at his head, and he fell on his knees, murmuring, 'I accept death for the name of Jesus and his Church.' Then Tracy struck again, and Thomas fell at full length with outstretched arms as if in prayer.[2] Richard Brito, who hitherto had not used his sword, now struck at the head of the dying archbishop so powerfully that the blow cut off the top of his skull, while the blade split into two as it struck the pavement.[3] Hugh de Moreville, the fourth, had been keeping the crowd back at his sword's point, and did not touch the archbishop, but Hugh Mauclerc, one of the followers of the knights, set his foot on the dead man's neck and scattered his brains on the stones with his sword-point, exclaiming: 'This traitor will not rise again'.[4] Then the knights, again shouting 'King's men, king's men', left the church for the cloister and the great court. Straightway Robert de Broc and others began to pillage the archbishop's lodging, breaking open cupboards and snatching up money, plate, vestments, precious cloths and papal bulls. Others ransacked the lodgings of the clerks and others again took the horses from their stables. The four knights rode back to Saltwood, where they went over the day's work, and Tracy claimed (in error) to have cut off the arm of John of Salisbury.[5]

In the cathedral the body lay as it had fallen. Thomas's body-servant, Osbert, cut off a piece of his own shirt and covered the mutilated head.[6] Then for a short time the archbishop lay all alone in the dark transept. The monks had been scattered by the men-at-arms and were then occupied in clearing the people out of the desecrated church and locking all the doors. When they returned to the dead archbishop Robert of Merton, his confessor, showed those around him the hairshirt, which even his own clerks had never seen, beneath the monastic habit and the canon's rochet that he was wearing. The hairshirt and drawers were sewn tightly round the body and thighs, but could be opened at the back for the

---

1. W. FitzStephen, *MB.*, iii. 141. It is impossible to be certain of the number and order of the blows. E. Walberg, in *GW.*, pp. xcv–xcvi, endeavours to sort them out.
2. *MB.*, iii. 141–2.
3. *MB.*, iii. 142.
4. E. Grim, *MB.*, ii. 438.
5. William of Canterbury, *MB.*, i. 134.
6. W. FitzStephen, *MB.*, iii. 146–7.

daily scourging. The whole garment was alive with vermin,[1] and the monks remarked to each other that the martyrdom by sword was more tolerable than this other never-ceasing martyrdom. The night was stormy, with thunder,[2] while the monks washed and dressed the body and laid it before the high altar, praying in silence, since no solemn office could be sung in the church polluted by bloodshed.

Next morning Robert de Broc arrived and, calling the monks together, threatened them that the corpse would be thrown to the dogs unless they buried it secretly. They, therefore, buried the archbishop in the crypt, having taken some of the clothing and bloodstained cloths from the pavement as relics. Within a few days reports and tales of signs and wonders began to pour in, the first trickle of a stream that was to put Canterbury in the front rank of European shrines of pilgrimages, and to carry the story of Thomas's last hour all over Christendom in glass and stone and illuminated page.

1. E. Grim, *MB.*, ii. 442. 'Bestiunculis obsitum'; Anonymous II, *MB.*, iv. 134. 'Pediculorum multitudo'.
2. The only authority for the thunderstorm is the eyewitness William FitzStephen (*MB.*, iii. 142–3). His language is rhetorical but the statement seems clear. He goes on to describe a glow in the sky—*rubor aeris magnus* —which critics who trust the words rather than the intention of the writer suppose to have been aurora borealis.

L

CHAPTER II

The Aftermath of the Murder

NEWS OF the murder in the cathedral spread rapidly and provoked a spontaneous cry of horror all over Europe. We may compare the reaction with that of the world of our own day to the assassination of President Kennedy. For six years all the courts and churches of western Europe had followed the contest of principles and personalities between the king of England and his archbishop, and it is probably true to say that the sympathies of the majority lay with Thomas. His mistakes and seeming faults of character are clearer to posterity than they were to his contemporaries, who knew him only by repute, while the great achievements of Henry II in the legal and administrative spheres, which appeal to the modern mind, had little attraction for his subjects, and still less for continental observers, who were more concerned with his acquisitive designs against themselves or their neighbours. Most men would have thought of Thomas only as an archbishop forced to flee from his church and his country, and living in seclusion and penance with the loss of all his revenues. To them he must have seemed the David to Henry's Goliath, who was struggling, not principally for himself, but for the Church—the Church of Canterbury and then the Church of Rome or, quite simply, for the Church. To this sympathy were added the place and manner of his death, which seemed clearly to add the lustre of martyrdom, a judgment soon confirmed for that age by the miracles of healing. Canterbury became almost overnight the Lourdes of its world.

For Henry it was, for the moment and the immediate sequel, a disaster. A graphic account of his distress, carefully attuned to the ear of Alexander III by Arnulf of Lisieux, never the most truthful of mortals, shows the king clad in sackcloth and ashes, shut up in his private room, lamenting and refusing food.[1] It

1. *MB.*, vii. (738), 438–9.

was the natural reaction of an extrovert temperament to a shock
of any kind. Even from Arnulf, however, we gather that the
king was as sorry for himself as for the archbishop, fearing he
might be held responsible. The bishop of Lisieux, therefore,
begged the pope to punish the criminals and clear the reputation
of the innocent king. Henry himself wrote at the same time,
blaming the archbishop for his seditious activity and laying the
murder at the door of those who had been excommunicated by
his violence. It was they who had, Henry regretted to say, killed
him. He himself had, indeed, spoken angrily about the archbishop
some time ago, and although his conscience was clear his reputation was in some danger. Would the pope help him with some
good advice about this?[1]

Alexander, however, was not prepared to rescue Henry's
reputation. Shortly before Christmas the king had sent out
John Cumin and Master David, Gilbert Foliot's trusted and
trustworthy agent, to seek absolution for the suspended and
excommunicated bishops. They arrived in January, and negotiations were going favourably when the news of the murder came
through, followed by a clutch of letters—from King Louis, from
the archbishop of Sens, and from others, all demanding vengeance.[2]
Alexander felt the shock deeply. Like the king, he shut himself
up for a week and gave a general command that no Englishman
must come near him.[3] He had, indeed, seen more than enough
of them in the past few years. The envoys sent by the king had a
difficult journey and many misadventures, but they arrived
about Palm Sunday, a numerous and ill-assorted team of whom
the bishop of Worcester, who had been absent from the coronation, was the most powerful. The going was heavy, and despite
the support of five or six cardinals it was generally supposed that
Henry would be excommunicated and his lands interdicted on
Maundy Thursday, the traditional date for such announcements.
The envoys spread money freely about and by engaging themselves
on behalf of the king to obey any future papal mandate they

1. *MB.*, vii. (739), 440. 'Et (quod dicere sine dolore non valeo), occi-
derunt . . . Quia . . . plus famae meae quam conscientiae timeo, rogo . . .
ut . . . me salubris consilii medicamine foveatis.'
2. *MB.*, vii. (734-5), 428 ff.
3. *MB.*, vii. (751), 476. 'Generaliter interdictum est ne Anglici ad eum
haberent accessum.'

achieved partial success. The interdict on Henry's continental dominions was confirmed; the king was forbidden to enter a church and legates would be sent to look into the case. In addition a comprehensive anathema was launched against all who had taken part in, or aided in any way, the murder of the archbishop.[1] Shortly after this, Alexander, who had seemed obdurate towards 'the Gilbertian trinity', as he called them, gave permission for the archbishop of Bourges to absolve them if the legates failed to arrive within a month of the return of Gilbert's envoys.[2] The archbishop died within a week of the commission, but in the event the legates arrived in good time. Before they came, however, Henry, who had received disquieting news of the conduct of Richard de Clare in Ireland, took the opportunity thus offered of disappearing from an awkward situation. Meanwhile, Bartholomew of Exeter was given complicated instructions how to deal with the various categories of guilty men who in one way or another had incurred canonical penalties in England.[3]

The king remained at a distance till he was recalled early in 1172 by the threatened revolt of his sons, and, as before, impending catastrophe drove him to seek peace with the Church. He declared himself prepared to meet papal envoys. The legates duly arrived and met the king at Savigny on 16 May, but Henry was truculent and would not swear to do all that the pope might command him. He must leave again for Ireland, he said, where urgent calls for him were being made.[4] Six days later, however, he thought better of it, and at a conference at Avranches he swore to observe whatever the legates commanded, and while denying that he had either ordered or desired the murder, admitted that it had been done ostensibly for his sake and that his angry words and behaviour might have been a cause. Nevertheless, he maintained that sorrow rather than satisfaction had been his when he heard of the murder, and he glossed this somewhat neutral statement by adding that he had grieved less when his parents died.[5] Then, together with the young king Henry, he swore to a number of

1. *MB.*, vii. (750), 474.
2. *MB.*, vii. (752), 480. 'Vos et trinitatem vestram (sic enim dominus papa loquitur)'. The trinity were presumably Gilbert, Roger and Jocelin.
3. *MB.*, vii. (780), 534–6.
4. *MB.*, vii. (771), 514. 'Redeo in Hiberniam, ubi multa mihi incumbunt.'
5. *Ibid.*, 'audita morte ejus plus inde doluit quam laetatus est'.

undertakings. The first was, never to depart from the obedience of Alexander III. Then, (a) he was to provide two hundred men for one year for the defense of Palestine, and to take the cross himself within three and a half years. This promise was later commuted to the foundation of three religious houses. (b) He was to restore to the see of Canterbury all its lands, churches, etc., just as they were at the time of archbishop Thomas's exile. (c) He was to restore his favour and their possessions to all those, clerics and lay people, who had been deprived of them for their kinship with Thomas or support of his cause. (d) He was to allow appeals to Rome in cases of ecclesiastical jurisdiction, though the king might ask assurance that no injury was intended towards him. (e) He promised to abrogate the customs established during his reign that were damaging to the Church.[1] He later glossed this in a letter to Bartholomew of Exeter with the remark that he could not think of any such customs.[2] The last four of his promises were in effect answers to the demands that Thomas had made before his return, though there was no explicit renunciation of the Constitutions of Clarendon. The agreement at Avranches was confirmed by Alexander III on 2 September, and in the bull announcing this the pope added that the bishops' oath at Clarendon was void.

The canonization of the archbishop, for which the murder would have cried aloud even had signs and miracles been lacking, was declared by the pope on 21 February 1173.[3] A year later, in July 1174, Henry crossed from Normandy to England in a tempest, and did public penance at Canterbury, where, after a night's vigil at the tomb of the martyr, he asked for pardon and was scourged by the whole community of monks, an incident that was commemorated in stained glass and illuminated manuscripts by the generation that followed.[4] This gesture was the king's reaction to the outbreak of the great rebellion of his sons and their allies, and it had its due effect, in the king's opinion and that of his friends, when the king of Scotland, invading England, was taken prisoner at Alnwick on the day the king left Canterbury.

1. *Ibid.*, 514 ff.
2. *MB.*, vii. (773), 519. '[Consuetudines] quas quidem aut paucas aut nullas aestimo.'
3. *MB.*, vii. (783), 544 ff.
4. Gervase of Canterbury (RS). i. 248–9.

When Henry had restored order in England and his dominions overseas, a further stage of negotiations developed, and a legate *a latere*, cardinal Hugo Pierleone, was in the country for several months in the winter of 1175-6. He obtained several further concessions from the king. The first settled the contentious question of criminous clerks, which had been avoided at Avranches, and the settlement was made on the lines demanded by archbishop Thomas, with the exception, unpopular in the country, of clerical transgressions against the forest laws. Henceforward no clerk was to be taken before secular judges for any crime or forfeiture save against the forest law, or in the matter of lay service for a lay feoff. Moreover, the murderers of clerks were now to be tried in the king's court and deprived of all possessions in addition to any previous sentence.[1] This arrangement, so far as it concerned the trial of clerks, was taken up by Alexander III *circa* 1177 in a letter to the king of Sicily which became the decretal *Licet praeter* with its paragraph *At si clerici*. The king also agreed not to hold the lands of vacant bishoprics long, save for exceptional circumstances, and to allow canonical elections in his chapel.

When we remember that Henry was acting from what would for a less able king have been a position of extreme weakness, we may think that he had made a remarkably successful recovery. He had, indeed, abandoned the claim to try and punish criminous clerks, but the very fact of his yielding on this point may suggest that the loss to justice and to social morality was less than had been suggested at Clarendon, and in fact the matter does not bulk large in any list of charges against the clergy before Tudor days once more made it fashionable. Indeed, if the Church had restricted exemption to those in major orders, neither society nor equity would have been the worse for the freedom allowed; it was the inclusion of a large and partially disreputable class of tonsured clerks that provided matter for a charge of scandal. On other matters the final result differed little from the run of procedure in the later years of Henry I. There was, however, an important if indefinable difference between the situation in 1177 and that in the years immediately before Clarendon. Henry

---

1. R. Diceto (RS.), i. 410. The relatively small extent of Henry's withdrawal is discussed by H. Mayr-Harting in the *Journal of Ecclesiastical History*, xvi. (1965), 39–53. But England remained within the papal jurisdiction in a way that William I did not experience.

in those early years was attempting to replace a regime of negotia-
tion and opportunism on the part of both king and bishops by
one of rigid decree in favour of the king. Thomas met this by an
equally rigid demand on behalf of canon law and papal procedure.
Now, in fact, flexibility was restored without calamitous difference
to either party. Certainly Henry in his last years acted more freely
than canon law allowed in elections and prohibitions. On the
other hand, canon law was implicitly recognised as having a
status, and reasons had to be shown, or at least devised, for
breaking it. In feudal and monarchic Europe the exact and
permanent execution of canon law would have been a moral
impossibility, but this is not to say that the requirements of
canon law could never be observed. The simple fact was that
neither canon law nor the constitutions of Clarendon were
practical politics. It was not a matter of State versus Church as
in the Roman Empire or the modern world. It was, rather, that
two authorities, both acknowledged, at least so far as words went,
by the whole population, claimed control of the activities of that
population. In an ideal world a division and separation of jurisdiction might have been conceivable. In the world as it was—
and is—the overlapping of rights and the extravagant claims
of both sides ensured perpetual controversies. The German
Henry IV in the eleventh century, and the English Henry II in
the twelfth made the same kind of political error that the
Italians Boniface VIII and Sixtus V made in their later days.

CHAPTER 12

The Case Reviewed—
Henry II, Gilbert Foliot,
Alexander III, Archbishop Thomas

IN the previous chapters of this book an attempt has been made to present the complicated and often controversial career of archbishop Thomas as it is seen in a narrative of the events, with as little comment as possible on the wisdom or probity of the actors. Yet the attraction which the episode has always had for the reader of history lies precisely in the challenge it offers to our perception of political wisdom and moral worth. This challenge, and the difficulty of meeting it, is present in this controversy with an urgency that is found in no other episode of English history before the reign of Henry VIII. Quite apart from the dramatic interest of the story, the number of unusually gifted men of complex character who were involved, and the quantity of biographical and other documentary material to be considered, combine to give an intellectual interest both to the story itself and to the task of disentangling the series of events and of forming a judgment upon the chief characters.

It has seemed allowable, therefore, in this concluding chapter for one who has over the years approached this controversy and its sources more than once, to give with some freedom his judgment on the characters of the story, and on the political and religious interests that were involved. Four groups of men, each with a leader of exceptional powers, were involved: King Henry with his ministers and allies; Gilbert Foliot with his fellow-bishops; Alexander III with his cardinals and curia; archbishop Thomas with his supporters. We will look at these four in turn.

We have seen on an earlier page the impression that the king made upon some of his contemporaries. He was on any reckoning an unusually gifted man, with an unusual combination of qualities, good and bad. Had there been no 'Becket affair' in his reign, his character might have seemed less complex and he might have appeared as a wiser king and a better man. His later misfortunes with his sons and their mother might have been attributed to their failures in larger part than to his. Indeed, until very recently the controversy with Thomas overshadowed all else in accounts of his reign. In more recent works we can find a long account of his judicial and administrative reforms with scarcely a mention of the great controversy we have been studying, and without question the king of one side of the picture is different from the king of the other. The two images in our mind are, indeed, not easy to harmonise, and it is this that lends something of tragedy to our conception of Henry. Thomas was fated to expose a facet of Henry's character, a heartless and shifty facet, that another archbishop of Canterbury might have left unseen.

The young Henry undoubtedly admired Thomas. He was attracted and stimulated by him both in council and in lesiure. Nevertheless, the relationship was always one of master and minister. Henry was an egoist, not with the all-consuming egoism of a Henry VIII or a Napoleon, but in the sense that neither as king nor as man did he defer to, or learn from or consider the interests of others. A contemporary remarked that he was unchanging in his love and in his hatred when once they had found an object. Archbishop Thomas would seem at first sight to demolish this judgment, but it may be suggested that Henry never loved Thomas with sincere personal affection, but was attracted by his more superficial qualities of comradeship, versatility and efficiency. When these were no longer at his service, enmity took the place of amity. Henry's sudden outburst at Fréteval: 'Oh, if you would only do what I wish', is very revealing. Once friendship had changed to hostility, the darker side of Henry's character appeared. Besides the unwisdom of setting the ancestral customs down in writing, there was the greater fault of allowing his passion to obscure his political wisdom. Instead of realizing that he was set on a collision course with a body of law and sentiment which might be adapted, but could not be obliterated, he turned all his violence against the person and possessions of the archbishop. In the struggle that followed he appeared shifty, unreliable and obstinate. Yet he remained a king who could draw from John of Salisbury in the very heat of the quarrel a tribute of praise as the equal, if not the superior, of his fellow monarchs in Europe, one of whom was the brilliant Frederick Barbarossa.

No king of medieval England had an abler group of servants than Henry. We shall never know how much the clerks of the exchequer and others in the royal service contributed to produce the ideas or the initiatives in the legal and administrative reforms of the reign, but we may remember that for many years the king was abroad, and therefore all the work and many of the decisions were left to the clerks and the justices at home, and that for many years Henry was on a knife-edge of policy, when a mistake could, and did, result in excommunication for himself and an interdict for his subjects. That on the whole he 'got away' with so much for so long, was at least partly due to the skill and persistence of the clerks who defended his cause in the Curia, as they had executed his designs in the exchequer or on the bench as justices— John of Oxford, Richard of Ilchester, Richard FitzNeal and others. That they were not mere functionaries, but took a lively and intelligent interest in the king's work, is seen clearly in Richard FitzNeal's *Dialogue of the Exchequer*. We must beware of giving too much weight to the descriptions of these men and their allies as 'devils of the king's court'. Many of them became in due time bishops and founders of religious houses. Much of the rivalry between the households of Theobald and Thomas and the king's court was party rivalry, such as exists between, let us say, leading members of the Government and Opposition in Parliament at the present day. Both parties looked to make their way by patronage, and the passage was easy from one group to the other.

Henry himself, with all his talents and qualities and achieve-ments, lacks the clear light of greatness, perhaps because he seems to lack that coordinating and directive quality that we call wisdom. He is not a statesman of the calibre of William I, who, despite his harsh and ruthless actions, pursued and achieved aims that were governed by considerations higher than mere opportunism or efficiency. Henry II, like Henry VIII, though perhaps less consciously, kept his counsel to himself. No personal or intimate letters of his have survived, if indeed they were written, and we have no speech or manifesto to tell us how far, if at all, he realised the significance of his constitutions and his assizes. He was an extrovert, and in some ways apparently at the mercy of his passions. All agree that he was quite untrustworthy where his own interests were concerned. Yet he was the friend and patron of saints, in particular of Gilbert of Sempringham and Hugh of Lincoln. He was certainly aware of religion and feared external religious sanctions, though considerations of piety and morality had seemingly little influence on his conduct. At least, we may say that he stood within the framework of religion; he did not professedly scout it or disbelieve in it; but his attitude towards its demands was formal rather than spiritual. In the last resort, we have the impression that his implacable opposition to the archbishop was that of a hard and frustrated man with a strong opponent who thwarts him, with the additional bitterness of a selfish and revengeful man towards one who had slighted him by following what he claimed to be higher principles.

The bishops as a body, though not if considered as inconsistent and erratic individuals, can be seen in retrospect to have been potential arbiters of the dispute. Had they all throughout stood firm against the king it is hard to see how he could have overcome their resistance. Though they were, as barons, his men, he could not, in the society of his day, have eliminated them. He had no weapon such as the Tudor *Praemunire* nor would such a weapon have had the same effect. In the twelfth century the papacy still had the last argument. On the other hand, had they all accepted his demands and never moved from their oath at Clarendon, it is hard to see how a solitary archbishop could have won through. That they were vacillating and divided was due to variety among them of character and moral strength. That they were not submissive to the bidding of a king was due to the strength of the ideas of the Gregorian reform. In their attitudes they reflected the outlook of a particular epoch. Fifty years earlier Anselm stood almost alone for the papal programme. Neither under Henry I nor under Stephen would the bishops of England as a body have recognised the force of canon law as against the king's prerogative, still less would they have recognised the compulsive force of obedience to their metropolitan. This pull of loyalties has not been sufficiently realised: the pull of loyalty to the king and his (in many ways) reasonable demands, and the pull of obedience to the archbishop and pope as regulated by canon law.

The attitudes adopted by the various bishops at various times have been discussed elsewhere; the story is too complicated to be resumed here. Looking back on what was written twenty years ago, I would only add that the readiness with which the bishops, especially the senior bishops, accepted the leadership of the *parvenu* ex-chancellor so soon and so simply, seems to me very remarkable. In part it may have been due to the compulsive influence which Thomas undoubtedly had over the men of his day, but it was due still more to their consciousness of involvement as bishops in the interests of the Church as a whole. In particular, the steady influence of Henry of Winchester, the 'real grandson of the Conqueror',[1] against the actions of his nephew, is very striking. But he did not stand alone. Had Thomas possessed the tact and persuasive eloquence of a great politician, he could have held the whole group of bishops in a solid phalanx of defence.

One bishop stands alone as deserving notice in any review. Gilbert Foliot, if we omit the ageing, *çi-devant* Henry of Winchester, was undoubtedly the ablest of the bishops and the one of highest repute. He had had long administrative and pastoral experience as abbot of Gloucester and bishop of Hereford. He was a preacher and an ascetical leader of note; he was also an expert canonist, especially in procedural matters. When Theobald died he must have been regarded, and must have regarded himself, as a strong candidate for the succession. We have his own words to tell us that he disapproved greatly of the worldly conduct of chancellor Thomas, and of his concessions to custom and to royal avarice in such matters as exploiting episcopal estates when the see was vacant for a long while.

The case for and against Gilbert's conduct during the eight years 1162–70 has been debated at great length, both in the past by Robertson, Froude and Freeman, and in recent years by Dom Adrian Morey and Professor C. N. L. Brooke and myself,[2] as well as by expert reviewers of our books, and a rehearsal of all the relevant evidence has been made so fully and fairly by Brooke and Morey that it would be tedious and unnecessary to go over the whole field again. In the past much has depended upon the attitude of the individual writer to archbishop Thomas. Hagiographers abused Gilbert; Protestant historians defended him.

1. R. H. C. Davis, *King Stephen*, London 1967, 127.
2. *GF.*, 147–87.

In recent years there has been some agreement in the assessment of Thomas, though complete agreement is probably unobtainable, since the ultimate judgment is one of spiritual values. Foliot, however, still remains a figure of controversy. Twenty years ago, in some lectures which were later published, I spoke harshly and perhaps rhetorically of him. It was natural and right that some of these judgments should have been questioned at the time by Professor R. W. Southern, and should since have been fully and critically examined by Morey and Brooke. In the course of that examination a new charge emerged, that of complicity in the forgery of charters when Gilbert was abbot of Gloucester. I will leave aside this charge, which rests on exact scholarly calculations and is on a different level from those connected with the great controversy. Where then do we stand?

The main counts of the indictment against Foliot can be reduced to six broad headings. That he hoped for the archbishopric and opposed the election of Thomas for this reason. That, when translated to London, he refused to swear obedience to him and later attempted to raise London to metropolitan rank to avoid submission. That he turned against him after Clarendon and showed bitter hostility towards him at Northampton and thenceforward. That he was the leader and inciter of the opposition among the bishops throughout the period of exile. That he wrote a series of hostile letters, culminating in the celebrated *Multiplicem*, in which much unjust abuse and historical inaccuracy are to be found. That, finally, by assisting at the coronation of the young king, he violated what he knew to be the just claims of Canterbury, as well as the papal command and by taking his grievances immediately to the king helped to precipitate the final tragedy. This list, which by no means exhausts the crime-sheet, is a considerable one and its cumulative force is strong. In most respects the actions or words are not in question, but a defence has been made somewhat as follows.

Foliot's dislike of Thomas and his opposition to his appointment were at worst only natural and at best wholly justifiable; in background, personality, career and conduct, Thomas was born to be an offence to the ascetic, balanced, intellectual and conventional monk, abbot and bishop. Foliot's refusal to take (or repeat) the oath of obedience was not novel, and was in the event approved by the pope; his hopes of raising London to metropolitan status were likewise not new, and had at least an arguable case behind them. When the troubles began he rapidly saw more clearly than Thomas that the best, indeed the only, way of avoiding a disastrous impasse was to go some of the way with Henry, in the spirit of the concessions made by Anselm and later by the papacy at Worms. It might then be possible by perseverance and diplomacy to soften the offending clauses of the constitutions of Clarendon. When Thomas showed himself as obstinate as the king, Foliot decided that resignation or deposition of the archbishop was the only way out. After that, one thing led to another and Foliot, like so many who try to hold to the *via media*, found himself under fire on all sides and used his expert knowledge of canon and Roman law to evade ecclesiastical disaster, till towards the end of the controversy he became genuinely uncertain which way to go. His letters, though undoubtedly bitter, partizan and inaccurate, are understandable in the circumstances, and are matched in bitterness and inaccuracy by those of the archbishop.

As testimonials in Foliot's favour, we have the panegyric of the abbot of Cluny,[1] the personal letter of praise from Alexander III[2] and the judgment of all responsible for his rapid advance from post to post, and then, when peace had returned to the Church, the testimony of Walter Map to his honourable and active old age.[3] Against him, we have the enduring accusations of the archbishop, who had taken every possible step to bring about harmony after his election; of John of Salisbury who, for all his critical spirit and committed position, must be accounted the finest and most cautious mind in public life at the time; and the judgment, held in some cases many years after the event, of all Thomas's biographers and a wide range of his other supporters.

From all this, if a personal judgment may be allowed (and no other sort of judgment is possible), we would seem to be justified in concluding, first, that the beginning of the feud of collision of minds and wills, came from Foliot. Granted that he had had extremely bad fortune in the Canterbury election, the new archbishop showed himself ready not only to forget the stiff opposition that Foliot had put up, but to give, by the translation to London, what compensation he could to a sore and defeated

1. *MB.*, v. (20), 30–2.
2. *MB.*, v. (26), 42–4.
3. *De nugis curialium*, i. 12, cited *GF.*, 72.

rival. Had Gilbert, in the sequel, given no more than passive submission to the king, there is no reason to suppose that the archbishop would have shown more hostility towards him than he showed, let us say, to Hilary of Chichester. Secondly, that although many of Foliot's actions can be defended individually as comprehensible or even excusable, the final impression that most readers of all the available sources carry away is that of a bitter, cold and in some ways devious enemy of the archbishop, who uses questionable arguments and procedural expedients to preserve his freedom of action. In the whole controversy the spirit of tolerance and the milk of human kindness are in short supply on all sides, but nowhere is the deficit more evident than in the acts and words of Foliot.

Yet the apparent dilemma remains. How are we to explain the apparent, not to say real, contrast between the 'image' of Foliot both before and after the episode of Thomas's archbishopric, and the impression he gives between 1162 and 1170? The historian as such cannot give an answer. All he can say is that before 1162 and after 1170 Foliot appears as a man of probity and good repute, performing his official duties duly and honourably, whereas between those dates his words and actions raise a series of doubts and questions. We have not even the assistance that the careers, let us say, of St Augustine or Napoleon give us, the one by a slow but visible moral and intellectual conversion, the other by a slow deterioration of a sense of ethical and social responsibility under the influence of ambition. The Foliot of the late 'seventies is apparently a reappearance of the character of twenty years before. There the historian must leave it.

But anyone who has lived with Foliot, on and off, for many years cannot help himself but he must set this man, of whom we know so much, against his own experience of men in literature, in history, and in life. Searching thus, he may think that the evil in Foliot, if evil there was, must have been of an intellectual kind that has little apparent influence upon the outward show of a man. There is an uncommon, but not imaginary, type of character, in a man possessed of unusual mental powers and a natural good judgment in social life and professional work, who cannot abide a possible rival, however unconscious or blameless that rival may be, and who pursues that rival's path with implacable enmity. The Gospel story shows us the supreme example of such a type. There, too, we see men who, before and after their searching trial, pursued a distinguished and to all appearances an honourable career. In life's common experience the contrast between the parties is less marked, and elements of good and ill may be seen on either side, but the radical psychological tension is a real one. On this showing Foliot's genius was rebuked by one who, without any of his own ascetic practice and monastic observance and expert conduct of spiritual affairs, had suddenly, by illicit favour and with all the faults of a parvenu, passed him in the career which was reaching its climax, and had become one to whom he now owed spiritual and practical obedience.

By contrast to Henry and Gilbert Foliot pope Alexander III is a simpler subject. His problem, though it had spiritual implications, was primarily a political, diplomatic one. For part of the crucial period he was an exile from his see and his native country, with an old colleague enthroned as rival against him, his own city either in revolt or occupied by his enemies, and the whole Empire in schism. Even though he had won the king of France as a faithful ally, the king of England, lord of half of what is now France, was hesitant even in the peaceful years before 1162, and could subsequently use the threat of schism to counter any papal threat of sanctions. It is natural that English historians, few of whom in the past have been interested in papal history, should have concentrated their attention solely on the pope's treatment of Henry and the archbishop, and this, considered by itself *in vacuo*, has a superficial resemblance to the vacillations of weaker popes such as Clement VII. It is possible, indeed probable, that Thomas, who knew his king well, was justified in thinking and saying that Henry would always retreat at the crack of the whip and that the threat of excommunication and interdict would bring him to heel, but we may remember that Thomas himself baulked at Vézelay in 1166 and at other times, and left the king untouched, and we may feel that the pope, badgered by the archbishop and plied with counter-arguments by cardinals who favoured Henry and by the king's emissaries, may be excused for his unwillingness to stake all on a throw that might end in disaster. Moreover, he was well aware of the ability and reputation of Foliot, and an old friendship bound him to Jocelin of Salisbury. Doubtless, could wishes have worked wonders, Alexander would have consigned both Henry and

Thomas to the thermal waters of Bath,[1] but to do him justice the pope never went back on his condemnation of the Constitutions of Clarendon or on his support of the archbishop's principles. As so often happens in papal history, his immediate advisers the cardinals were divided in their allegiance and it may be that English gold, so often in the past a powerful ally of English diplomacy, made its weight felt. Taken for all in all, however, Alexander was a pope of great courage and administrative ability, and at the end of the day, before the final scene, he had the grace to acknowledge that the archbishop's judgment on Henry was correct. Alexander had the care of the whole of the western Church, schismatic emperor and all, and he was ultimately to win through to unity and a large measure of peace. To those who study his whole pontificate—the longest on record since St Peter's—his courage and care for discipline and order, even in his most desperate moments, will excuse his apparent indecision during the exile of archbishop Thomas.

And what of Thomas himself? In previous chapters an attempt has been made to keep to narrative without comment, but everyone who writes or reads the story of this great quarrel must form his opinion as to its rights and wrongs, and as to the conduct of its protagonist.

We may begin by drawing attention once more to his racial origin. Both mother and father were Normans by locality of birth and, if related to Theobald, the likelihood is that his father was a northman also to some extent by blood. Thomas, therefore, may be expected to show some of the characteristic traits of a Norman, the kin of the Conqueror's barons and bishops, the cousin of the *conquistadores* of Apulia and Sicily, and not those of Wulfstan of Worcester or Ailred of Rievaulx or even Anselm of Aosta. Those traits are courage, ability to lead men, extroverted energy and administrative ability, joined to a harshness, lack of subtlety and human sympathy, and a formalised outlook in matters of religion. By and large we can see these traits in Thomas.

Whether or no he had a simpler character than Henry and Foliot, he is more readily estimated on the spiritual level, partly because it is the level on which he wished to live throughout

1. To which John of Salisbury consigned the prior of Bath (*MB.*, vi. (367), 334). ' Ille vester collega Batoniensis, qui utinam submergatur in thermis, quibus dignus est.'

his life, and partly because his was a more frank and open nature than that of Henry or Foliot. His judgment may at times have been at fault and his conduct reprehensible, but he was willing to admit this in the long run. He does not hide his feelings or mince his words. Two important decisions in his career have caused divergence of judgment upon him. The first was his acceptance of the chancellorship, which he held as a post in which he submitted all his talents and his judgment to the service of Caesar rather than of the Church. The second was his acceptance of the archbishopric with an even more determinate resolve to devote all his efforts to the service of Christ. It has already been suggested that the manner of his action and the energy which he put into his service were manifestations of one and the same character, that of a strong, extroverted, greatly gifted and fundamentally simple personality, whose nature it was to go straight forward along a chosen path without considering alternative policies or the reactions of others. Behind this character was the spirit of a man who saw from early days that he must give all his strength to the service of God, but who also saw the splendours of the world of men and felt his power to shine among them. Like many another, he yielded to the attractions of place and power, and was driven far off the course which he knew was the true one, leading thus a divided, and fundamentally dissatisfied, life. When, beyond all expectation, he was offered a charge which was in every sense a challenge both to his natural ambition and to his conscience, he accepted it, after his manner, with both its splendours and its sacrifices. He could now be himself, no longer at war within, but his conversion was not the result of patient striving or of a sudden illumination, and he carried into the new life some of the loyalties, the tastes, and the weaknesses of the past. Whatever may have been the deficiencies in Henry's character and capacities for deep feeling, Thomas had deep emotions and loyalty, yet at the same time he must convince himself and others that the season of indecision and self-indulgence was past. He must show the king and all others that he stood for the rights of the church, the Church of Canterbury, the Church in England, and the Roman Church, to the last ounce of his strength. Hence the note of stridency in his penances, in his display and in his assertion, sometimes needless and gratuitous, of the rights of the Church against the king. He slipped more than once, and felt the burden of the course he had taken, but each time he came back more fiercely eager. And both at Woodstock and at Northampton he saw that Henry had lost whatever personal affection he might have had for him. Both on the human level and on that of principle it was a war in which one must lose all.

At various moments of his life Thomas made errors of judgment and showed flaws of character. It was probably a serious error in human relationship to pit himself against the king immediately after his election on matters that were essentially secular. It was an error in political judgment, however correct he may have been in technical, legal lore, to act so brusquely in the matter of criminous clerks before Henry had pondered over the matter. It may be that discussions took place of which no record survives; it may be that he judged, and judged rightly, that nothing would move Henry and that the best defence was to take the offensive, but in view of Henry's actions at other times and with other opponents there would seem to have been at least a possibility that tact and diplomacy might have succeeded better than a direct challenge. On the other hand, he was certainly guilty of indecision and vacillation at Westminster and again at Clarendon. There, and at other moments of his career, he did his cause great harm by taking his decisions and acting upon them without taking counsel or even informing his colleagues. Such actions roused both resentment and distrust, but the trait was built into Thomas's character and he never eradicated it, nor, seemingly, did he ever acknowledge it as a fault. It is evident on crucial occasions during his exile, notably at the Vézelay censures of 1166 and in the acceptance of Henry's terms at Fréteval in 1170, and it can probably be seen in his conduct at several of the earlier conferences of that time. It appeared for the last time in the conversation with John of Salisbury immediately before the murder.

Thomas was to blame also, in the eyes of many readers of his story, for precipitate and violent action, particularly in his excommunication of John of Oxford and Jocelin of Salisbury, and in that of the bishops on the eve of his return, and of his enemies on Christmas Day 1170. Even if it is said that he had been justly angered by the failure of Alexander to take decisive steps previously, it is not clear that these censures aided his cause in any way. And it might be said that he struck at the servants, but not at their master. Similarly, both in his letters to Gilbert Foliot and elsewhere, he used a violence of language which has a personal bitterness which is absent from the fiercest denunciations of St Bernard, to say nothing of mis-statements which it is not easy to attribute to his reputedly faultless memory.

These and, perhaps, other faults may be justly urged against him. On the other side, we may allege his undeniable moral and physical courage. When he failed, it was not from fear of personal loss or injury, but from a mistaken loyalty or affection, or at least a mistaken judgment of Henry. When his foe was visible, whether at Toulouse or Canterbury, he faced him and death without flinching. Moreover, his fortitude in exile and in the physical suffering he endured or inflicted upon himself was unshaken and admirable, as was his steady refusal to abandon his principles or to imitate the king in his transports of fury or in his flagrant dishonesty. Of his inner spiritual life we see little, either in the story of his doings or in the letters to or from his friends. It is a tribute to his greatness, and also to his basic nobility of mind and heart, that he was able to retain the presence and the affection of a very distinguished group of men for six years in trying circumstances, when any of them could have had advancement at court had they been willing to join the few who defected. Moreover, several of those who, although not members of his household, remained his faithful allies, were men of high ability and integrity, such as his old colleague John of Poitiers, Henry of Rheims, King Louis's brother, and above all, John of Salisbury. John differed greatly from the archbishop in gifts and character and in the whole cast of his mind; nevertheless, he steadfastly endured an exile on his own account and remained throughout the years an advocate and counsellor of untold value, on account of both of his intrinsic worth and integrity and by reason of the high esteem in which he was held at the papal and French courts, and by all who knew him. John is the principal link between the two worlds that rarely touch each other in the story, that of archbishop Thomas and the English and French courts, and that of the schools of Paris and Chartres, of Peter Lombard and Richard of St Victor. John, who in other phases of his career appears sometimes as a fastidious, almost cynical intellectual, critical of several of the enthusiasts and saints of his day, is seen in his letters to the exiles as a wise and constant friend, able to stand aside and criticize or deprecate, but in essentials solidly with the archbishop and convinced that great principles were at stake. Great as was his admiration for King Henry, even after the experience of his disfavour, and greatly as he must have longed for the life that might have been his, he may on occasion have counselled moderation of tone and action, but he never counselled appeasement.

Of all the decisions of archbishop Thomas, that taken at Fréteval in 1170 is, perhaps, the hardest to explain. It has been said that he failed either in his judgment or in his strength of purpose, as he failed at Westminster and Clarendon, either through weariness or from a combination of loyalty and personal affection. It has been said, alternatively, that it was the action of an *exalté*, bent upon being a martyr, and his reputed words, uttered on more than one occasion and cited by Herbert of Bosham, giving his conviction that only death could end the controversy, are quoted in favour of this view. Perhaps both may contain a partial, but far from complete, element of truth. Thomas had never lost his affection for Henry, nor had he lost his care and loyalty for the king whose servant and vassal he still was, *salvo ordine suo*. On the other hand, by 1170 he had clearly approached to a view of the controversy as one concerning the very life of the Church in England, and one which, like a tragic drama, could be resolved only by death. Yet there is plenty of evidence that he rejoiced in his return to Canterbury, and looked forward to a new lease of life there, and there is no action, apart from the decision at Fréteval, which suggests a sense of fatality. Perhaps the years of penance and frustration had killed in him all hope of a final and satisfactory concord with Henry, and had also strengthened him to accept whatever might come. He may have felt that all further negotiations would be endless and useless, and that he must break the deadlock at all costs. True, a letter to the pope suggests that he believed a genuine arrangement had been made, but this may be no more than a manifesto to be made public, while the deeper conviction remained unexpressed. Certainly the evidence of words and acts in the last two months of Thomas's life shows a conflict between two levels of experience. On the surface the exhilaration, the display, the denunciation; beneath this, a solemn expectation of the end.

A final question has often been asked, or answered, by historians Was Thomas in any sense a saint, apart from his death, when this is adjudged a martyrdom? If a clear answer 'Yes' or 'No' must be given, it must be negative. Had Thomas returned to Canterbury and enjoyed a year's normal life before succumbing to a stroke, there would have been no miracles, no bourgeoning of biography and presumably no canonisation. The two exiled archbishops who achieved that honour, Anselm and Edmund Rich, though they were not martyrs, were venerated as intrinsically holy at every phase of their lives, and had no questionable episodes to live down. Thomas, on our interpretation of his acts, had never been an immoral man, but he had certainly acted against his own ideals, whether from ambition or from human respect, and had caused scandal and harm to the Church by so doing. Later, after his election, he had publicly failed on more than one occasion to hold to his principles. That he repented of all these actions, and did what to modern eyes seems hard penance for them, is true, but this of itself does not imply sanctity, though it may prepare for it. And even if we credit him with a high degree of fortitude and constancy in his exile, with its penances and its trials, we are still not wholly satisfied. A saint who is not a martyr must show in fair measure something of all the virtues of Christ—lack of self-seeking, gentleness along with fortitude, generosity and love in word and work, equanimity and self-control in every difficulty. Not all these qualities are visible in Thomas, even in his last months and days. Perhaps the most we can say, as external spectators, is that he had fully atoned for his past failures, but had not yet shown all the virtues of a perfectly integrated sanctity.

Was his death, then, that of a martyr? If we use the word in its original Christian sense, we must say 'No'. He did not die as a witness to the Resurrection of Jesus, or in defence of any specified article of the creed or point of Christian morality. It has, indeed, sometimes been said that he died for a novel extension of canon law, or to recover Canterbury property, or because he had upheld an unessential right of the archbishop of Canterbury. All these, and other matters, formed some part of the large issue of rights which he was defending, but neither individually nor as a group were they the crucial point at issue. That, reduced to its simplest terms, was the demand of the king to treat the affairs of the Church, apart from its credal and sacramental aspects, as under his sole juris-diction. This was less, and far less explicitly conceived, than the demands that Henry VIII was to make. It was less than Charle-magne had made, without meeting with protest or opposition. But it was more than could be allowed in the religious climate of the twelfth century. A resurgent and a reorganized Church could not function under such conditions. Henry II failed both as a statesman and a politician in demanding agreement under oath to a return to the conditions that seemed tolerable enough in the reign of the Conqueror. He was unwise to hold fast to his demands even to the extent of taking the first steps towards leading his realm into schism. We may well think that some kind of a retreat would inevitably have taken place, if not in his reign, then under that of a successor. But as things were, in the predicament which both sides had combined to produce, Henry's demands could not be acceptable either to pope or to archbishop. Archbishop Thomas, at that particular moment, and in the largely accidental circumstances that brought about his murder, died for the freedom of the spiritual authority of the Church, and he died declaring that he knew this and was willing to meet death in this cause.

Note on the Biographical Material

The following is a list of the biographies written by contemporaries, given in chronological order so far as this is ascertainable, but the dating is often, at best, only probable or approximate. The figure given after each name is the volume of the Rolls Series in which the work is published.

WILLIAM OF CANTERBURY (i) wrote between June 1172 and December 1174.

EDWARD GRIM (ii) *circa* 1172.

GUERNES DE PONT-SAINTE-MAXENCE completed by the end of 1174.

WILLIAM FITZSTEPHEN (iii) wrote 1173-4.

JOHN OF SALISBURY (ii) wrote between April 1173 and July 1176.

ANONYMOUS II ('of Lambeth') (iv) wrote 1172-3.

BENEDICT OF PETERBOROUGH (ii) completed 1174.

ANONYMOUS I (Roger of Pontigny) (iv) wrote 1176-7.

ALAN OF TEWKESBURY (ii) completed by 1179.

[ROBERT OF CRICKLADE completed by 1180].

HERBERT OF BOSHAM (iii) completed 1186.

THÓMAS SAGA 1200-1250.

WILLIAM OF CANTERBURY was clothed as a monk and ordained deacon by Thomas in December 1170. He was present at the martyrdom and was subsequently a custodian of the shrine. His first work was a collection of the early miracles (printed after his *Life*). His *Life* may be taken as reflecting most accurately the tradition of the Canterbury monks.

EDWARD GRIM, a clerk of Cambridge, arrived at Canterbury to see the archbishop only a few days before his death. He was present at the murder, when he gallantly attempted to shield the archbishop and was severely wounded. He clearly took pains to investigate his subject and gives many facts of Thomas's early life. His work conveys an impression of sincerity and good judgment which suits well with his loyal and courageous conduct and the esteem in which he was held.

GUERNES, or GARNIER, was a French clerk who had seen, but had not known, the archbishop. He had visited Canterbury and learnt much from the monks, besides calling upon Mary, Thomas's sister, then abbess of Barking. He has provided many details, some of which appear nowhere else, and while occasionally embroidering his narrative with statements that cannot be checked, is nevertheless a valuable witness.

WILLIAM FITZSTEPHEN was a clerk and scribe of Archbishop Thomas at Canterbury, taking part also in the cases judged by the archbishop. Though he did not join the exiles, and made his peace with the king, he returned to Thomas's service in 1170 and was present throughout his last hours. He subsequently returned to the king's service and was possibly sheriff of Gloucestershire and itinerant justice. His work, by reason both of its literary qualities and its factual abundance, is the most important and attractive of the biographies.

JOHN OF SALISBURY, from whom a masterpiece might have been expected, gives only an outline of Thomas's early life together with a sketch of his character and the controversy. His almost contemporary letter describing the murder (MB., vii (748), 462-70) is likewise surprisingly uninformative. It has been shown that in his Life he even takes some of his facts and phrases from other biographers. Contemporaries, as well as modern historians, have deplored this reticence, of which the explanation is, perhaps, to be found in John's character and literary preferences or, it may be, in some personal circumstance in his life, connected with his appointment at Chartres.

ANONYMOUS II, whose work exists in a single manuscript at Lambeth, was later a monk of Canterbury, and says he witnessed the murder, but he adds nothing to the narrative of that event, and is in general the least interesting of the biographers.

BENEDICT OF PETERBOROUGH, monk of Canterbury, prior of Christ Church (1175) and later abbot of Peterborough (1177), wrote a short account of the martyrdom which contains a few details of first hand information.

ANONYMOUS I, probably written by Roger, a monk of Pontigny. He is very well informed on the details of the archbishop's wanderings from Northampton which he may have taken down from Thomas himself at Pontigny. It has been shown that he is indebted to Guernes for some of his material.

ALAN OF TEWKESBURY was a canon of Benevento before returning (later than 1170) to become a monk at Canterbury and, in 1179, prior there. In 1186 he was elected abbot of Tewkesbury. His *Life* covers only the period between the council of Clarendon (January 1164) and the conference of Montmirail (January 1169). Alan is the most scholarly of the biographers and quotes considerably from the collections of documents which, as we shall see, he had made. Moreover, Lombard, one of the most eminent of Thomas's household in France, became archbishop of Benevento in 1171, and Alan may well have derived information from him.

ROBERT OF CRICKLADE, prior of St Frideswide's, Oxford, *c.* 1140–*c.* 1180, is known to have written a *Life* which has disappeared. It was certainly used by the author of the Icelandic saga (see below), who preserves some details from it.

HERBERT OF BOSHAM, clerk and confidant of Thomas from his consecration onwards, was a man of parts, a scriptural scholar of note and well versed in canon, and perhaps also in Roman law. He was a bold and radical supporter of the archbishop, and could face Henry II in a long green surcoat, without a qualm. All readers have noted his deplorable volubility and self-conceit, but he stood very near to Thomas, though he missed the martyrdom; and while the speeches he reports must be largely his own inflated recollections, his records of Thomas's behaviour and *obiter dicta* are probably reliable. All in all, he must stand next to FitzStephen in importance and interest among the *Lives*. Though he wrote long after all the others, he makes no use of them, and is sometimes demonstrably at fault in his dates and places. Even so, his mistakes are clearly simple lapses of memory, and are not due to partisanship or flights of imagination.

THÓMAS SAGA ERKIBYSKUPS. This, an Icelandic saga, dating in its present form from the early fourteenth century, was edited by Eiríkr Magnússon (RS., 2 vols., 1875–83). It is based upon the *Life* by Robert of Cricklade and supplies several personal details about the archbishop.

The relationship between the biographers, and their dates of composition are difficult questions, and many attempts have been made to disentangle the evidence, notable by L. Halphen, 'Les Biographes de Thomas Becket', in *Revue Historique*, cii (1909), 35–45, and more fully and successfully by E. Walberg, *La tradition hagiographique de St Thomas Becket avant la fin du xiie siécle*, Paris 1929. Walberg's findings have been accepted by most subsequent writers, such as R. Foreville and D. C. Douglas, and have been used above.

Taken as a group, the biographers give a clear impression of factual fidelity. They were all members of a sophisticated class, who had lived through great events and had known many of the actors, great and small. They were not writing in a remote cloister, nor using sources uncritically. Though all were writing of a sainted world-hero, and thus in a sense prejudiced, they do not draw upon their imagination, nor do they use the *clichés* of hagiography catalogued by Père Delehaye in *Les légendes hagiographiques*. Save for a few youthful incidents in Thomas's life, which are probably family folklore embroidering actual happenings, and later prophetic utterances which may well be the forebodings of a sensitive and farsighted mind, there are scarcely any traces of the miraculous such as tax the modern reader's credulity even in the biographies of Bernard and Francis. Partly, no doubt, this is because all but eight years of Thomas's adult life were notoriously deserving of criticism rather than admiration; partly, also, because the shower of posthumous miracles freed the biographers from the necessity of amassing proofs of sanctity. This general sobriety makes the patently sincere emotion of John of Salisbury, at the exhibition of wonders before his eyes at Canterbury in 1171, all the more impressive (*MB.*, vii (748), 462–70).

The biographical and hagiographical material (Miracles etc.) take up vols. i–iv of the series of seven volumes that make up the *Materials for the History of Thomas Becket* (RS., 1875–85), all of which were prepared and published by Canon J. C. Robertson except the last, which was seen through the press by his colleague Dr J. B. Sheppard. This has rightly been called by Professor D. C. Douglas (*EHD.*, ii. 698), a 'major work of scholarship', and constant reference over many years has confirmed the present writer in his admiration for it. Robertson had long been steeped in the documents in manuscript and earlier editions, and his life of *Becket* (1859) still remains valuable by reason of its detailed narrative closely tied to the documents. Robertson greatly assisted future critics of his work by his own candid assessment of its limitations. He had not always been able to revisit manuscripts to examine them in the light of his own increased knowledge, and he recognised that the chronological order of the documents was often uncertain. Moreover, he was hindered by the standing orders of the Master of the Rolls, which only Stubbs openly disregarded, that long introductions and all save the briefest footnotes were prohibited. Cross-references, identifications, discussion of questions of dating, and the like, such as are expected as a matter of course from a modern editor, are scanty or non-existent. Consequently, the reader who suspects an error in arrangement has often to spend much time in reading and re-reading a whole series of letters. While the text is usually sufficiently accurate for all ordinary purposes, subsequent research has in individual cases provided a fuller text and accurate dating. Before a complete and accurate account of the years 1164-70 can be written, a thorough examination of the whole correspondence is essential.

The magnificent series of documents edited in *Memorials* is principally due to John of Salisbury and Alan of Tewkesbury, who made a collection of all the pieces they could lay hands on at Canterbury, arranging them as best they could in chronological order. This collection makes up some two-thirds of the three volumes of letters in *Materials*, the rest coming from collections of Becket and Foliot documents in the Bodleian Library, Oxford, with other less important MSS. elsewhere, and a few additions from the letters of John of Salisbury and others. Some account of these various sources is given by Morey and Brooke, *Letters and Charters of Gilbert Foliot* pp. 17 ff.

Besides the lives and letters of the *Materials*, some details, events and judgments can be obtained from the extant Pipe Rolls, from the early letters of John of Salisbury, and from the chroniclers such as Gervase of Canterbury, Ralph of Diceto (who was present at the Council of Northampton), Roger of Howden, William of Newburgh, and Gerald of Wales. Such topics as the criminous clerks have of course a technical literature of their own, of which a good summary is given in the article by Dr Charles Duggan used in the relevant chapter of this book.

Modern works

Of the numerous modern lives of St Thomas, only three or four are of any assistance to the student or historian; the others give only a short narrative or develop a particular thesis for or against the archbishop. Thomas Becket was one of the many topics on which J. A. Froude and E. A. Freeman came into prolonged and sometimes acrimonious conflict, and their writings are often of great literary brilliance, while many of Freeman's judgments are valuable. Robertson's *Becket*, excellent for its date, has already been mentioned. In the same year as Robertson, Fr J. Morris, S. J., published his work of hagiography, *Becket, the life and martyrdom of saint Thomas of Canterbury*, which in its second edition (London 1885) remains the best life of its kind. For Thomas's early life, *Thomas of London before his Consecration* by L. B. Radford, is a work of unusual excellence. The author, a schoolmaster and clergyman, made use of all the available printed sources, and since these have increased very little since his day, the work retains its value after almost eighty years. The author's judgment was good, and his scholarship faultless. The book has been out of print for more than half-a-century, and is only to be found in large or old libraries, and as it stops precisely where the general interest in the subject begins, it is unknown even to many medievalists, but those who know it have been saved many an hour or day of research by the long and well-chosen extracts from the sources in the author's footnotes.

In the past fifty years only one major work on Thomas has appeared, that by Raymonde Foreville, *L'Eglise et la Royauté en Angleterre sous Henri II Plantagenet*, Paris 1943. This, a book of more than 600 pages of close print, is on any showing a notable achievement, which might seem to attain the status of a definitive work, but when it became available in England it met with only limited approval. This was partly due to the planning of the book, which may have owed its amplitude to the author's inexperience, for it was an early work in Mlle. Foreville's career. It covers the whole age from 1066 (and earlier) to the end of the twelfth century and is, thus, an awkwardly large book for one who is interested only in the archbishop and his years of controversy. Moreover, by covering such a wide field, the book was liable to be overtaken in many sections by the intensive study of the Church and feudalism in England that began immediately after World War II. Finally, Professor Foreville had a surer touch with institutions than with personalities and movements of sentiment, and her warm espousal of the cause and character of Thomas, and her prejudice against Henry II and Gilbert Foliot, which are not supported by thorough analysis, and in particular her treatment of the letter *Multiplicem*, which she regarded as a squib, possibly composed by John of Salisbury, tend to falsify the picture she draws. It was unfortunate that her chapters covering the same period, in Fliche et Martin's *Histoire de l'Eglise*, ix, 2, should have been written almost at the same time as the larger book, though not published till 1953.

Nevertheless, Professor Foreville's work should not be neglected. Her familiarity with all the sources is impressive, and in particular when dealing with canon law she was well in advance of most English scholarship of that day, and she anticipated in part the conclusions of Dr Duggan and Miss Heslin mentioned in the text above. Certainly, for my own part, after re-reading Professor Foreville's work after more than twenty years, I found my respect for her scholarship and detailed knowledge greatly increased.

Nine years or so ago, when I undertook to write this short biography, it would have been true to say that no recent work of the kind existed. Since then Richard Winston has published a book of almost exactly the same scope (*Thomas Becket*, London 1967). Had this appeared before I engaged myself for the task, I might well have declined to undertake it, but, as it was, I felt that I must go forward, despite the many good qualities of Mr Winston's book.

The following works, most of which have been mentioned in the footnotes of this book, bear closely on the subject, and may be recommended to any who wish for further reading.

Z. N. Brooke, *The English Church and the Papacy*, Cambridge 1931.

C. R. Cheney, *From Becket to Langton*, Manchester 1956.

R. H. C. Davis, *King Stephen*, London 1967.

W. H. Hutton, *St Thomas of Canterbury*, 2 ed., London 1899.

C. Johnson, *Dialogus de Scaccario*, London 1950.

M. D. Knowles, 'Archbishop Thomas Becket: a Character Study', (British Academy Lecture, 1949), reprinted in *The Historian and Character*, Cambridge 1963.
The Episcopal Colleagues of Archbishop Thomas Becket, Cambridge 1951.

A. Morey, *Bartholomew of Exeter*, Cambridge 1937.

A. Morey and C. N. L. Brooke, *Gilbert Foliot and his Letters*, Cambridge 1965.

A. Morey and C. N. L. Brooke, (edd.), *The Letters and Charters of Gilbert Foliot*, Cambridge 1967.

K. Norgate, arts. in *DNB.*, on Henry II, Thomas Becket, and several other contemporaries of note.

A. Saltman, *Theobald, Archbishop of Canterbury*, London 1956.

W. Urry, *Canterbury under the Angevin Kings*, London 1967.

C. C. J. Webb, *John of Salisbury*, London 1932.

Index

Individuals appear under their personal names, save for the Becket family. Throughout TB = Thomas Becket. B. = Benedictine. C. = Cistercian. No attempt has been made to note all occurrences of Thomas Becket and King Henry II.

LEADERS OF RELIGION

GENERAL EDITOR: C. W. Dugmore, DD
Professor of Ecclesiastical History, University of London

A series designed to provide a basic history of Christianity in Britain and
among British people overseas by means of biographies of churchmen
notable for their contribution to the development of the Christian religion
in this country or representative of some phase or movement within the
Church.
Each volume, complete in itself, contains biographical detail to place the
subjects in their own environment, but the authors' main concern will
be to assess their contribution to the complex strands forming the pattern
of Christianity through the centuries.

―――――――

Already published

AUGUSTINE OF CANTERBURY *by Margaret Deansley*
THOMAS BECKET *by David Knowles*
HUBERT WALTER *by C. R. Cheney*
HENRY CHICHELE *by E. F. Jacob*
WILLIAM TYNDALE *by C. H. Williams*
RICHARD BAXTER *by Geoffrey F. Nuttall*
JOHN WESLEY *by V. H. H. Green*
JOHN WILLIAM COLENSO *by Peter Hinchcliff*
JOHN HENRY NEWMAN *by C. S. Dessain*

In preparation

JOHN WYCLIF *by James Crompton*
SIR THOMAS MORE *by T. M. Parker*
THOMAS CRANMER *by C. W. Dugmore*
EDMUND GRINDAL *by Patrick Collinson*
RICHARD HOOKER *by W. M. Southgate*
FRANCIS ATTERBURY *by G. V. Bennett*

431V10ᴹ 4278 H Group
09/10/13 320005 SELB